What Every Woman Should Know

Abdul Hye, PhD

Madina Masjid, Inc.
Houston, Texas

What Every Woman Should Know

Published by:
Madina Masjid, Inc.
815 Oak Harbor Dr.
Houston, Texas 77062
281-488-3191
abdulhye@hotmail.com

Printed in the United States of America

Library of Congress Catalog Card Number: 2002093030

ISBN 0-9668190-5-5

What Every Woman Should Know

Preface

All praise belongs to God. Everyone needs His guidance to become successful in this life and in the hereafter.

Life is moving very fast, especially in the West. Most women are busy with jobs and children, and have very little time to study religion and think about the life in the hereafter (where we have to live forever). The divorce rate is very high and continuously on the rise. Many times, after divorce, the women end up caring for the children and do not receive financial support or aid from their ex-husbands. Along with pregnancy, women have to deal with all of these new problems, which lead them to become overstressed, overburdened, and overworked. Most men, on the other hand, simply move from place to place, find a new mate, a new life, without any real commitments or responsibilities for their children or wives. This places most of the women into great hardship, financial burden, fatigue, and ultimate health breakdown. They go through seemingly impossible missions in trying to juggle all of their duties and responsibilities at the same time. They often try to find hope in religion and God. However, religious leaders often do not tell the complete truth about religion for fear of loss of members, especially those who provide financial support. They maintain their authority, monopoly, and influence by keeping the general public in the dark, confused and entirely dependent upon them. The general public, in return, pays dearly with a blind expectation that they will get the best deal from God in this world and in the hereafter.

The so-called feminist movement started in this country as late as the 18th century. It has made "progress" in the areas of equal rights, the workplace, and marriage. However, wife beating, harassment, and general disrespect are still rampant in this society. It can be safely stated that although this society has advanced equal rights *legally*, the reality has changed very little. The advancements remain mostly on paper only.

Islam, however, has dealt with the issue of women's rights very clearly and systematically. It has prescribed a means to dissemble the harsh and lude treatments towards women and has replaced them with a respectable and just alternative. Islam has furthered women's rights way before the idea of "feminism" was heard of. It quickly transformed the status of women from a lowly, destitute object to one of a respectable, upright, important part of society. It made strides in this area at a time when "feminism" or "equal rights" was unheard of, and it still upholds these principles even today.

Ponder, if you will, on the quality of life. How have the Western "rights" improved your status? Are you really free of injustice? Can you safely walk down the street? Are you free from harassment? Do you receive the right amount of respect? Do men still use you?

Consider, also, why you do the things you do. Do you dress a certain way because a male designer has told you that this is the latest fashion? Do you dress a certain way because society expects it from you? Do you find yourself competing to fit the standard of beauty set by men? Do you tolerate harassment to keep your job? Do you worry about your husband/ son having access to strip clubs or pornographic films, which humiliate and degrade women (which were also created by men)?

Consider, also, why Islam is viewed as the religion that is "unfair" to women. Are you feeling this way because of the way Islam is portrayed in the media? Have you had personal experiences with Muslim women? Are you basing your opinion on how you have been raised? On what your own culture promotes? And what makes you think that Christianity, Judaism, or any other religion is a feminists' paradise? Have you actually studied these religions? Take a moment to ponder these things; prepare to learn the **truth** about what your religion really says. Then, with an open mind, consider why **Islam is the ultimate ideal for women**.

This book is compiled with **true** information from the Old Testament (Hebrew-Torah), New Testament (Greek-Bible), Quran, and other Holy Scriptures to accurately present all the facts without any bias (without changing or making up false information). This should help an individual to understand what is at stake for the eternal life and how she can find the **truth** and make a rational choice. Life in this world is very short. It can stop at any time no matter how busy we are, whether we are prepared for it or not. This book should help anyone understand the basics of different religions, how they deviated from the truth, and how any woman can arrive at the final truth from God with the help of accurate information. It has already begun. Remember, nearly 4 out of 5 converts into Islam in the USA are WOMEN.

All praise belongs to God if anything from this book is used towards finding the truth. I ask forgiveness from God and from all of my readers if there is any mistake, in spite of my best efforts.

Abdul Hye, PhD
Houston, Texas
June 10, 2002

Table of Contents

Introduction

Women comprise <u>more than 50%</u> of the world population. But their rights and honor have <u>not</u> always been respected by the civilized society. Only recently, "equal rights" was given to women in the western society, usually in writing, but *not in practice*. Women are used mostly for physical pleasures and promotion of business. In the name of progress, equal rights and women's liberation, eventually women have been dragged down from the lofty and most respectable position given to them by God, to the most disrespectful position of "<u>object of pleasure and lust</u>". Women have been made to discard their graceful and honorable robes for something belittling and disgraceful. They have been humiliated and made to undress in public in the name of fashion, style, music, or fame by the so-called 'civilized' man. Only in the non-Muslim countries will one find things such as pornographic films where women are objects used and ranked by their physical bodies (not their minds!). Here, women are given the "freedom" to humiliate themselves. Is this what women's liberation is all about? In one pretext or another, women have been lured out from the protection of their homes to the open field, infested with hungry wolves, who start devouring them at the earliest opportunity and continue to do so till they are through using them. The result of this is manifold: crime, rape, murder, frequent divorce, domestic violence, miserable life, single parent homes, low moral and family values, abortion, prostitution, drugs, human-trafficking, loss of peace and instability in the society, etc. In order to take care of these social issues, civilized society is spending billions of dollars on police, law-enforcing agencies, jails, correctional facilities, hospitals, child custody, courts, attorneys, etc (to name a few).

<u>**Did you Know**</u> **that nearly 4 out of 5 converts into Islam in the USA are WOMEN! Here are some reasons....**

<u>**Testimonies of Women Who have Embraced Islam**</u>
http://thetruereligion.org/sisters

Name	Home	Prior Belief	Notes/Quotes
<u>Akifah Baxter</u>	FL, USA	Christian	**"I felt like all along I had been a Muslim"**.
<u>Amal</u>	USA	Catholic	**"The trinity was a lingering concern for me."**
<u>American</u>	USA	Catholic	**"I am a 17 year old Caucasian American girl.."**

Amina	Canada	Christian	"When Islam is practiced, it is a beautiful sight"
Amina Mosler	Germany	Christian	"God guides whom He pleases to the right path"
Aminah Assilmi	USA	Christian	"I couldn't be a Muslim! I was American and white!"
Amirah	AR, USA	Baptist	"..the words "terrorist lover" spray painted..". Her homepage
Amy Lea Reinking	USA	Christian	Her website is aimed at women.
Anja	Germany	Christian	A complete book on her journey to Islam. Also in Deutsch
Anonymous		Catholic	"Muslims are not people to be feared"
Asiya Abd Al Zahir	Australia	Christian	"..the only religion I have ever been completely sure of.."
Bushra Finch		Christian	".. I found unacceptable, particularly the idea of the Trinity"
C. Huda Dodge	USA	Catholic/ Presbyterian	"..I am truly happy and at peace.."
Carol		Christian	"I felt that my soul had been set free!"
Celine Ludic		Catholic	"..I now wear Hijab and I am very happy.."
Chahida Zanabi	Norway	Christian	"..I found [a belief that Jesus died] illogical and unjust". Homepage
Cheryl		Catholic	"..I had to asked Allah for forgiveness, there is no middle man.."
Dani	USA	Catholic/Buddhist/Pent.	"..I just knew that there is only ONE GOD"
Deanne	Australia	Christian	"Muslim girls that were somehow more liberated than I felt"
Elizabeth		Catholic	"Islam was the missing piece in my life"
Erin/Sumaya		Christian	"I was amazed at the scientific knowledge in the Qur'an"
Evangeline Do	Canada	Protestant	United Church of Canada. See the Vietnamese Muslims'

			Homepage
eye		Jehovah's Witness	"And everyday I thank Allah for letting me find Islam"
Lady Evelyn	UK		"Islam is the religion of common sense"
Fathima	South Africa	Pentecostal	"I turned to Allah and finally I found peace and tranquility"
Fathima Ranshiz	Philippines	Christian	"[Listening to] recitation of .. Quran I used to enjoy a kind of solace"
Fatima Kazue	Japan		
Former Missionary	Africa	Catholic	She was formerly a missionary! A revealing testimony!
Gabriela Pruneda	TX, USA	Catholic	"I never thought I would myself become a Muslim some day"
Hanifa	Ireland	Catholic	
Helena	Sweden	Protestant	"I was fed all the propaganda through mass media.."
Hudda Droll	USA		"I cried and I cried, thanking God for this precious gift.."
Iman		Lutheran	"It didn't take long for me to convert.."
Indrani	Singapore	Hindu	Indrana and her husband share their touching story.
Jade	Canada	Catholic	"I began to realize the many contradictions of the Catholic religion"
Jamilah		7th Day Adventist	"I had .. intentions of converting Muslims and I became converted"
Jemima Goldsmith	UK	Jewish	Daughter of billionaire Sir James Goldsmith
Jenni Rauhala	Finland	Christian	Her website about Islam, in Finnish
Jewellee	USA		"..the best thing I ever did in my life and I never looked back"
Joanne Richards	CA, USA	Catholic	"..embracing Islam has been the single greatest gift ever.."
K.H. Abdullatef	USA		"What kind of book was this?"

Kareema	MI, USA	Christian	"Why would God create himself in human form and die?"
Karen Flamiano	USA	Catholic	"If Jesus is God, then why did he have a conversation with God"
Dr. Kari Ann Owen	USA		"I began to look .. to Islamic culture for moral guidance"
Karima		Secular Humanist	"..I have found the door to spiritual and intellectual freedom"
Karimah		Southern Baptist	"..one never actually heard the whole Bible - only select verses"
Kathy	Canada	Atheist	"I was once a happy 'speculative atheist'"
Khadija	Ireland	Catholic background	"I felt really sure that there is no God but Allah"
Khadija			"..God Almighty in His Infinite Mercy answered my prayers"
Khadija	Philippines	Catholic	"Teresita converted to Islam? What got into her?"
Khadijah		Catholic	"I am a better person today and I have faith in my Allah"
Khadijah Watson	Now Saudi Arabia	Christian	Former pastor, missionary, professor. Master's Degree in Divinity
Lara	Canada	None	"I find Islam ever-more fascinating, and I enjoy living as a Muslima"
Laure	France	Buddhist	"I was afraid to be seriously wounded"
Leila Raffin	Paris, France	Catholic	"Islam has a very bad image in non-muslim countries.."
Lori	OH, USA	Christian	"If Jesus was God than how could Jesus (God) die on the cross?"
Lyla	CA, USA	Quaker background	"I felt so peaceful and happy"
Madonna Johnson		Christian	"..all of my turmoil and anxiety was gone.."
Mahasin		Jehovah's Witness	"..we would knock on doors on Satuarday mornings.."
Mahmuda	Australia	Catholic	"..I had always been a Muslim

			without being aware of it"
Malaak	VA, USA	Christian	"I knew that *the things in the Qur'an had to be from Allah*"
Mary Abdalla	MA, USA	Catholic	"I was determined to find something wrong with Islam". Homepage
Maryam	Egypt, USA	Catholic/ Buddhism	"There is no more conflict within, because I have come home"
Maryam bint Noel	Australia, UK	Baha'i Faith	"I began to find Baha'i theology to be not quite honest". E-Mail her !
Maryam Jameelah	USA/ Pakistan	Jew	Formerly Margaret Marcus. Well known writer. Letter to her parents
Mas'udah	UK		"No .. religion .. have I found so comprehensible and encouraging"
Mavis B. Jolly	UK	Church of England	"..influenced by the usual condemnation .. I picked on polygamy"
Melanie	TX, USA	Christian	"..my heart screamed that this is the missing piece to the puzzle!"
Michelle	USA	Catholic (Jewish)	"I wish all mankind could come to know the truth (haqq) of Islam"
Michelle Al-Nasr			"..Islam, is my way of life, my love, my peacefulness, and my hope"
Monica	Ecuador/ USA	Catholic	"Islam, in contrast to Catholicism, seemed very pure"
Muslim Sister	USA	Christian	"You're American? Oh, your husband must be from the Middle East"
Nadia	USA	Christian	
Noor	UK	Hindu	Insights into Women in Islam vs. Women in Hinduism
Nourallah			"..I found my happiness in islam.."
Nur Habiba		Christian	"I am now 15 and wearing hijab and niqaab, subahaanallah"

Phreddie	USA	Christian	"I studied Islam quietly, on my own, in secret, for two years"
Qadirah			"I stated that all muslims were like the NOI.."
Rehana	USA	Southern Baptist	"I found the hijab very liberating"
Rosalina	Philippines		"I am now on the right path of life"
Rukaiya	Japan	None	"[Islam] was simple and logical .. never against human conscience"
Ruqayyah	USA	Christian	".. Islam doesn't teach that Jesus (P) was crucified"
Ruqqayah		Baptist/ Catholic	"how can three be one and the same?? "
S.S. Lai	Brunei/ UK		Chinese idolatry/ancestor worship
Sabrina C	Sri Lanka	Catholic	
Sabyrah Altagh	USA	Christian	
Safiyah Johnson	WI, USA	Christian	"After 48 hours I knew .. that I had found what I had searched for"
Sandra	USA	Christian	
Sara		Christian	"reading [truth about Jesus] was like having a light bulb turned on"
Shakira Graham	CA, USA	Christian Reformed	"I thought Islam was oppressive to women and .. terrorists"
Shannon		Christian	".. viewing Jesus as a Prophet .. makes a lot more sense"
Shariffa Carlo	USA	Christian	Some articles by this sister, on various aspects of Islam
Sharon Canaan	TX, USA	Christian	"WHY DO I HAVE TO GO THROUGH JESUS?"
Shellie Perreault	MI, USA	Christian	"I tried .. to find a valid argument for Christianity but I couldn't.."
Sigrún Valsdóttir	Iceland	Evangelical Lutheran	Her homepage about Islam

Name	Country	Background	Quote
Sophie Jenkins	UK	Catholic/ Protestant	"I was so angry, when I saw a Muslim woman in the street..."
Sumaiya (Kristin)	USA	Catholic background	"Accepting Islam was like an awakening of my spirit, my mind.."
Summaya	Canada		"[Islam] is widely assumed to be prejudicial to [women]"
Susannah	USA	S Baptist	
Themise Cruz	USA	Christian	"They think that we are fundamentalists or terrorists"
Tena	Canada	Anglican	"My husband read Qu'ran and then shortly after converted"
Tina	IL, USA	Protestant	"I thank Allah(swt) every day for guiding me.."
Um Kalthum			"I wear my hijab everywhere & no one makes me feel bad"
Um Luqman	USA	Catholic	"Jesus (P) made sense to me as being a Prophet"
Valerie N. Fields	NC, USA	Christian	"I had problems accepting Trinity", it didn't make sense"
Vera Ferrell	GA, USA		"My husband should be the only man to gaze upon my body.."
Yoko	Japan		"My mother wept and asked me to reconsider"
Z. Amatullah	PA, USA	Baptist	
Zaakira		Christian	"I can't explain how good I feel on the inside as well as the outside"
Zahirah		Catholic	3 of her siblings also embraced Islam !
Zahra Cox		Christian	"I feel so fortunate and blessed to have been guided "
Zahida	USA	Christian	"Allah guided me to the path of righteousness"
Zainab	USA	Christian	"No a guy did not convert me". An ex-Sunday School teacher
Zakiyyah	Australia		"..That one experience of salat [prayer] had a profound effect"
Zehra		Christian	"Allah had made the perfect religion, and I'd found it"

Western Society on Women

At a time when the media is incessant in its attempts to defame and ridicule Islam and the 'Muslim Woman', portray her as oppressed, abused and worthless, the following facts should be enough to prove that **western societies** are actually the ones worthy of the same accusations they throw at others:

Violence Against Women in the USA:

Domestic Abuse: http://www.letswrap.com/dvinfo/stats.htm

1. Approximately **95%** of the victims of domestic violence are women. (Department of Justice figures)

2. Every **9** seconds in the USA a woman is assaulted and beaten.

3. **4,000,000** women a year are assaulted by their partners.

4. In the USA, a woman is more likely to be assaulted, injured, raped, or killed by a male partner than by any other type of assailant.

5. Every day, **4** women are murdered by their boyfriends or husbands.

6. Prison terms for killing husbands are **twice** as long as for killing wives. (Why do men have lesser punishments?)

7. **93%** of women who killed their mates had been battered by them.

8. **67%** of women killed their mates to protect themselves and their children at the moment of murder.

9. **25%** of all crime is wife assault.

10. **70%** of men who batter their partners either sexually or physically abuse their children.

11. Domestic violence is the **number one** cause of emergency room visits by women.

12. Women are most likely to be killed when attempting to leave the abuser. In fact, they're at a **75%** higher risk than those who stay.

13. The **number-one** cause of women's injuries is abuse at home. This abuse happens more often than car accidents, mugging, and rape **combined**.

14. Up to **37%** of all women experience battering. This is an estimated **566,000** women in Minnesota alone.

15. **60%** of all battered women are beaten while they are **pregnant**.

16. **34%** of the female homicide victims over age 15 are killed by their husbands, ex-husbands, or boyfriends.

17. **2/3** of all marriages will experience domestic violence at least once.

18. Approximately **1,155,600** adult American women have been victims of one or more forcible rapes by their husbands.

19. Abusive husbands and lovers harass **74%** of employed battered women at work, either in person or over the telephone, causing **20%** to lose their jobs.

20. Physical violence in dating relationships ranges from **20-35%**.

21. More than **50%** of child abductions result from domestic violence.

22. Injuries that battered women receive are at least as serious as injuries suffered in **90%** of violent felony crimes.

23. In 1991, **only 17 states** kept data on reported domestic violence offenses. These reports were limited to murder, rape, robbery, and serious bodily injury.

24. In homes where domestic violence occurs, children are abused at a rate **1,500% higher** than the national average.

25. **50%** of the homeless women and children in USA are fleeing abuse.

26. The amount spent to shelter **animals is 3 times** the amount spent to provide emergency shelter to women from domestic abuse situations.

27. Family violence kills as many women **every 5 years** as the total number of Americans who died in the **Vietnam War**.

Workplace Statistics: http://www.capstn.com/stats.html

A telephone poll conducted by **Louis Harris & Associates** and released March 28, 1994 found that of the 782 workers polled:

- **31%** female workers claimed to have been harassed at work.
- **7%** male workers claimed to have been harassed at work.
- **62%** of targets took no action.

Of the women who had been harassed:
- **43%** harassed by supervisor.
- **27%** by an employee senior to them.
- **19%** by a coworker at their level.
- **8%** by a junior employee.

Of the women who claimed they had been harassed:
- **100%** of women = harasser was a man.
- **59%** of men = harasser was a woman.
- **41%** of men = harasser was another man.

Fatherless Homes: http://www.vix.com/pub/men/nofather/dart.html

Take a look at some statistics showing the effect the **ABSENCE** of a father has on nearly **22%** of American children in fatherless households:

- **63%** of youth suicides are from fatherless homes (Source: US DHHS, Bureau of the Census)
- **90%** of all homeless and runaway children are from fatherless homes.
- **85%** of all children that exhibit behavioral disorders come from fatherless homes (Source: Center for Disease Control)
- **80%** of rapists motivated with displaced anger come from fatherless homes (Source: Criminal Justice & Behavior, Volume 14, p. 403-26, 1978.)
- **71%** of all high school dropouts come from fatherless homes (Source: National Principals Association Report on the State of High Schools.)
- **75%** of all adolescent patients in chemical abuse centers come from fatherless homes (Source: Rainbows for all God`s Children.)
- **70%** of juveniles in state-operated institutions come from fatherless homes (Source: US Dept. of Justice, Special Report, Sept 1988)
- **85%** of all youths in prisons grew up in a fatherless home (Source: Fulton Co. Georgia jail populations, Texas Dept. of Corrections 1992)

In a country that preaches equal rights and propagates 'feminist movements', these statistics are extremely alarming. Shouldn't you ask yourself why, if the western ideologies on women are supposedly the true liberators, women are still suffering to this extent?

Domestic Violence in United Kingdom:

1. Domestic Violence accounts for a **25%** of all reported violent crime. (Working Party Report, Victim Support, 1992).
2. Domestic Violence is not limited to physical assault. It includes sexual abuse and mental cruelty, which undermine a woman's self-esteem. (McGibbon & Kelly,"Abuse of Women in the Home", 1989)
3. Research conducted by Police found that **2/3** of all men believed that they would respond violently to their partners in certain situations. (Islington Council, 1994).
4. Each year **100,000** women seek treatment in London for violent injuries caused in their homes. (Punching Judy, BBC-TV Doc, 1989)
5. Almost **50%** of all murders of women are killings by current or former partners. (National Working Party Report on Domestic Violence, Victim Support, 1992).

Crimes in Canada

Some people would tend to ridicule the whole argument of modesty for protection of women. Their argument is that the best protection is the spread of education, civilized behavior, and self-restraint. If 'civilization' is enough protection, then why is it that women in North America dare not walk alone in a dark street - or even across an empty parking lot? If education is the solution, then why is it that respected universities throughout USA have a **'walk home service'** mainly for female students on campus? Why do women carry self-protection items such as pepper spray or guns? Why do women take self-defense classes? If self-restraint is the answer, then why are cases of sexual harassment in the workplace reported on the news media every day? A sample of those accused of sexual harassment, in the last few years, includes: Navy officers, Managers, Priests, University professors, Congressmen, Senators, Supreme Court Justices, and even the President of the United States! Don't these people reach the level of "educated" or "civilized"? The following statistics, written in a pamphlet issued by the Dean of Women's office at Queen's University:

- In Canada, a woman is sexually assaulted every **6** minutes.
- **1 in 3** women in Canada will be sexually assaulted at some time in their lives.
- **1 in 4** women are at the risk of rape or attempted rape in her lifetime.
- **1 in 8** women will be sexually assaulted while attending college or university.
- A study found **60%** of Canadian university-aged males said they would assault sexually if they were certain they wouldn't get caught.

Something must be fundamentally wrong in this society. A radical change in the society's life style and culture is absolutely necessary. A culture of modesty is badly needed, modesty in dress, in speech, and in manners of **both men and women**. Otherwise, the grim statistics will grow even worse day after day and, unfortunately, **women alone** will be paying the price. Actually, everyone will suffer but as K. Gibran has said, "...**for the person who receives the blow is not like the one who counts them.**"

It is one of the great ironies of our world today that the very same headscarf revered as a sign of 'holiness' when worn for the purpose of showing the authority of man by Catholic Nuns, is reviled as a sign of 'oppression' when worn for the purpose of **protection** by Muslim women.

Common Views of Judaism, Christianity and Islam

From the time of the first human on earth (Adam (P)*), God has sent around 124,000 Prophets (chosen Messengers from God) to different places on earth at different times to guide **all** of mankind towards the one true God. The **same** God sent:

1. Moses (P) (about 3,300 years ago) with the Holy book: **Torah** (The Old Testament), which **Jews** follow under **Judaism**;

2. Jesus (P) (about 2,000 years ago) with the Holy book: **Bible** (The New Testament), which **Christians** follow under **Christianity**;

3. Mohammad (P) (about 1,400 years ago) with the Holy book: **Quran** (The Final Revelation), which **Muslims** follow under **Islam**.

Peace Be Upon Him

This book brings out only the truth from different religions (what is actually in each text). Judaism came from 'Judah', son of Jacob (P) (Israel), who was the son of Issac (P), who was the son of Abraham (P) through Sarah. Moses (P), a descendent of Issac (P), led his people and made them free from bondage under Pharaoh of Egypt. He lived 120 years and died somewhere in Sinai. Jesus (P) was a descendent of Issac (P), a devout Jew (Mark 1:35) born in Bethlehem. He preached and practiced the religion of Moses (P). "Christ" was not his name, nor was it Jesus (P). Jesus (P) is a Latinized version of the Hebrew name "Yeshua" meaning "God Saves". "Christ" comes from the Greek word Christos, which means "the annotated one". Jesus (P) lived 33 years and preached for four years. After he departed the world, St. Paul, who *never* saw Jesus (P), came about 70 years later, and reformed Christianity. Mohammad (P) is a direct descendent of Ishmael (P), son of Abraham (P) through Hagar. He was born in Makka on Monday August 29th 570AD and lived 63 years. He preached for 23 years, during which the Quran was revealed, and died in Madina in 633AD. All three prophets - Moses (P), Jesus (P), and Mohammad (P) are descendents of Abraham (P). In fact, when Abraham (P) died at the age of 175, both sons: Ishmael (P) and Issac (P) together buried him in Hebron, which still exists today. Mohammad (P) is the last prophet and his prophethood is for the entire world. He was illiterate (could not read or write), yet still delivered God's message (the Quran) as it was revealed. Islam (which can mean **"Peace"**) means submission to the will and law of God.

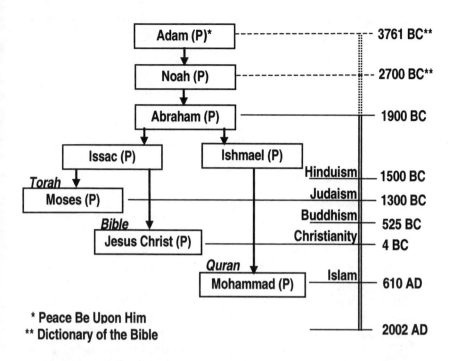

Muslims observe and maintain many instructions from the Torah and Bible

1. **Monotheism:** In the Torah, God says: "I am the first, and I am the last; and besides me there is no God" (Isaiah 44:6). In the Gospel, Jesus (P) says: "The Lord our God is one Lord" (Mark 12:29). The Quran says: "He is God, The One and Only" (Quran 112:1). **No Prophet ever claimed to be God and no Prophet ever said that there are more than one God.**

2. **Prophets**: Muslims believe and accept all the Prophets mentioned in the Torah, the Bible, and the Quran. A Muslim from his childhood is taught to respect each and every Prophet of God. A Muslim must add, "peace of God be upon him (P)" after pronouncing the name of any Prophet. Muslims show the highest reverence to Moses (P) and Jesus (P). God says: "We believe..which was revealed unto Abraham (P), and Ishmael (P), and Issac (P), and Jacob (P) and the sons of Jacob (P), and that which Moses (P) and Jesus (P) received...We make no distinction between any of them..."(Quran 2:136).

3. **Prophets with Exclusive Titles:** Although God anoints every prophet, they all have unique names. "Christ" (Hebrew-*Messiah*) is exclusive for Jesus (P). "Friend of God"(Arabic-*Khalilullah*) is associated with Abraham (P); "One who speaks with God" (Arabic-*Kaleemullah*) is

associated with Moses (P); "Messenger of God" (Arabic-*Rasulullah*) is associated with Mohammad (P). Muslims honor all prophets.

4. **Requirements of Faith:** Muslims accept Jesus (P) as one of the mightiest Prophets of God. It is not widely known that in the Quran, Jesus (P) is mentioned **25** times relating to his birth, mother Mary, his family, and activities. He is referred to as "The Word of God", "The Spirit of God", and the "Sign of God". There is not a single remark in the entire Quran that can be used against Jesus (P) (and thus should not offend any Christians). In fact, no Muslim is a Muslim if s/he denies what God says in Quran about Jesus (P).

5. **Miraculous Birth of Jesus (P):** Besides Christianity, Islam is the only religion on earth, which accepts the miraculous birth of Jesus (P) (that he was born without any father). (Quran 19:20). Many modern-day Christians do not believe in this today! Quran has two specific chapters #3 and 19 on Jesus (P) and Mary. When the angel informed Mary that she is going to have a son, the Quran presents the miraculous conception of Jesus (P) as:"She (Mary) said: 'O my Lord! How shall I have a son when no man has touched me (meaning sexually)?' He (angel) said: 'Even so: God creates what He wills. When He has decreed a plan, He says to it, 'Be' and it is!" (Quran 3:47). "The similitude of Jesus before God is that of Adam; He created him from dust then said: 'Be', and he was." (Quran 3:59).

6. **The Highest Honor of Women is Given to Mary, the Mother of Jesus (P) in Quran**: In the Quran, the angels say: "O Mary! Verily, God has chosen you, purified you and chosen you above the women of all nations."(Quran 3:42). There is also a chapter (#19) in the Quran that has been dedicated **in the name of Mary to honor her**. Out of 66 books of the Protestants and 73 of the Roman Catholics, not one book is named after Mary or her son, though you can find books named after Matthew, Mark, Luke, John, Paul, etc.

7. **Greetings:** From ancient times, the prophets of God including Moses, Joseph, David, Jesus (P), the angel of God and many others had customs to greet the believers with the words "Peace be with you" (Genesis 43:23, Numbers 6:26, Luke 24:36, John 20:19). Muslims greet each other with "Assalamualaikum" or Peace be unto you.

8. **Talking off Shoes:** God ordered Moses (P): " Moses, Do not come near; put off your shoes from your feet, for the place on which you are standing is holy ground" (Exodus 3:5). "And the commander of the Lord's army said to Joshua, 'Put off your shoes from your feet, for the place where you stand is holy" (Joshua 5:15). Muslims take off their shoes when they enter the mosque, a holy place of prayer.

9. **Washing and Purification Before Prayers**: "Moses, Aaron (P) and his sons washed their hands and their feet; when they went into the tent of meeting, and when they approached the alter, they washed; as the Lord commanded Moses" (Exodus 40:31-32). "Then St. Paul took the men, and the next day he purified himself with them and went into the temple" (Acts 21:26). Muslims wash and purify themselves before every prayer, five times a day.

10. **Humbling While Praying by Bowing Heads to the Ground**: "And he (Jesus (P)) said to his disciples, 'Sit here, while I pray'.... And he went a little further, and fell on his face, and prayed..." (Matthew 26:39). 'Bowing down to the ground' is also found in Psalms 95:6; Joshua 5:14; 1 Kings 18:42; Numbers 20:6; Genesis 17:3). "And... falling down on his face he will worship God, and report that God is in you of a truth." (1 Corinthians 14:25). "And Abraham (P) fell on his face: and God talked with him...," (Genesis 17:3). "And Moses made haste, and bowed his head toward the earth, and worshipped." (Exodus 34:8). Abraham (P), Moses, Jesus (P), and all prophets prayed with forehead on the ground in total submission to God. Muslims also bow their heads to the ground while praying.

11. **Not Bowing to Statues/Images:** "Thou shall not make unto thee any graven image, or any likeness of any thing that is in haven above, or that is in the earth beneath, or that is in the water under the earth: Thou shall not bow down yourself to them, nor serve them" (Exod.). Muslims do not bow to statues, images or anything except God.

12. **Fasting:** In the Bible, Prophets and people observed fasting (Act 13:1; Joel 1:14; Jonah 3:5). "And he (Jesus (P)) fasted forty days..." (Matthew 4:2). Muslims observe one month of fasting every year during the lunar month of Ramadan.

13. **Everlasting Covenant**: God made His everlasting covenants with Abraham (P) and his descendants: "Every male among you shall be circumcised" (Genesis 17:10,13). Abraham (P) was 86 when Ishmael (P) was born. Abraham (P) was 100 years when Isaac was born. Abraham (P) circumcised Isaac on the 8th day, as God commanded him (Genesis 21:4-5). "Add when 8 days were accomplished for the circumcising of the child, his name was called Jesus (P) (Luke 2:21). Muslims still keep this covenant; they circumcise their sons at birth.

14. **Abraham (P)'s Son Ishmael (P):** "...(Sarah) gave her (Hager) to her husband Abraham (P) to be his wife." (Genesis 16:3). "Arise, lift up the lad (Ishmael (P)), and hold him in thine hand, for I will make him a great nation." (Genesis 21:18). The name Ishmael (P) was chosen by God Himself: "And the Angel of the Lord said unto her (Hager):

'Behold, thou art with child, and shall bear a son, and shall call his name Ishmael (P), because the Lord has heard thy affliction." (Genesis 16:11). Ishmael (P) means "**God hears**." Muslims respect Ishmael (P) like Issac (P) as a son of Abraham (P).

15. **Wine Drinking Prohibited**: "For...shall drink neither wine nor strong drink.." (Luke 1:15). Muslims do not drink wine or alcohol.

16. **Pork Forbidden:** God ordered Moses and Aaron to forbid pork. "And the swine...is unclean to you. Of their flesh you shall not eat." (Leviticus 11:7). Jesus (P) never ate Pork in his life. Muslims do not eat pork.

17. **Abraham (P)'s Activities:** Abraham (P) took Ishmael (P) and Hagar and made a new settlement in Makka, called "Paran" in the Bible (Genesis 21:21), because of a divine instruction given to Abraham (P) as a part of God's plan. Kaba is the "House of God" built by Abraham (P) and his son Ishmael (P) in Makka for the worship of one true God. Muslims all over the world face towards that Kaba (as an act of unification) in order to pray. The spot where Abraham (P) used to perform prayers near the Kaba known as the "Maqam Ibrahim", i.e., the "**Station of Abraham (P)**" can be see today next to the Kaba. The ZamZam well (in Makka) created by Ishmael (P)'s feet (mentioned in Genesis 21:19) is still there for the last 4000 years and millions of Muslims drink this water throughout the year and take this water to every part of the world. The hills of Safa and Marwa (in Makka) where Hagar ran for water are located next to the Kaba. It is obligatory for every pilgrim (during Hajj) to run in the same way 7 times as Hagar did. The 3 places (in Mina) where Satan tried to whisper to Abraham (P) (who threw pebbles) while he was going with his son Ishmael (P) to sacrifice by God's order are still there. Every pilgrim is required to throw pebbles. Pilgrims in Makka and Muslims all over the world commemorate the sacrifices of Abraham (P) and Ishmael (P) by slaughtering an animal. Muslims are emulating these activities throughout the year.

18. **Usury/Interest Forbidden:** "Take thou no usury of him, or increase: but fear thy God; that thy brother may live with thee. Thou shall not give him thy money upon usury, nor lend him thy victuals for increase." (Leviticus). "He has put not out his money to usury, nor take reward against the innocent." (Psalms 15:5). Interest is forbidden in Islam.

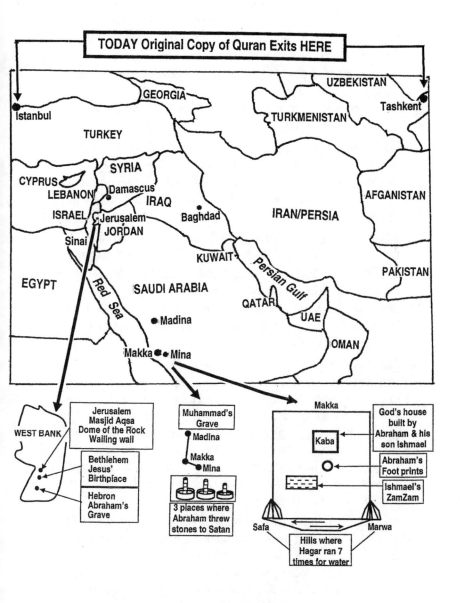

Holy places of Judaism, Christianity and Islam

19. **Disapprove Homosexuality:** "Then the lord rained upon Sodom and Gomorrah and fire came from the Lord out of heaven; and he overthrew those cities, and all the plain, and all the inhabitants of the cities, and that, which grew upon the ground" (Genesis). Homosexuality is forbidden in Islam.

20. **Decoration of Trees:** It is a heathen custom practiced during Christmas, and is forbidden in the Bible (Jeremiah 10:2-5). Tree decoration was borrowed from Pagan Romans and it is not a part of Jesus (P)' teachings. Muslims do not decorate trees.

21. **No Original Sin:** The Bible says: "The son shall not bear the iniquity of the father, neither shall the father bear the iniquity of the son: the righteousness of the righteous shall be upon him, and the wickedness of the wicked shall be upon him" (Ezekiel 18:20). Muslims believe that sin cannot be transferred or inherited from person to person.

22. **Accountability:** The Bible says:"...and every man shall receive his own reward according to his own labor." (1st Corinthians 3:8). Muslims believe that every person is accountable for his/her deeds and will get the reward accordingly.

23. **The Only Savior:** God said in the Bible: "I am the Lord; and besides me there is no savior'. (Isaiah 43:11, Hosea 13:4). Muslims believe that God is the only Savior.

24. **Alteration of Holy Books:** The Muslims believe in all of the original revealed holy books. The Bible says that no one should add anything to or take away anything from the Holy Book. (Revelation 22:18-19 and Deuteronomy 12:32). The Muslims believe that the Holy Books of God must not be altered. Man has repeatedly altered many Holy Books but no one has altered the Quran. Original copies of Quran still exist: one in Tashkent, Uzbekistan and one in Topkapi, Istanbul, Turkey. Today's Quran, word for word, is the exact copy of the original (Ref 12: p130-1).

There are many things that are common between the Jews, the Christians and the Muslims. Let us understand each other better and avoid all conflicts. Very soon, each of us will face God on the Day of Judgment, will have to give account for every action on this earth, and will face the consequences. Let us find the **Truth** and be prepared to accept it.

> **Judaism, Christianity and Islam have many things in common.**

Religious Scriptures

Human being needs guidance to be successful in this life and in the life hereafter. But their knowledge and ability are limited. Therefore man-made guidance cannot be perfect. Perfect guidance can *only* come from God who has perfect knowledge. Holy Scriptures are guidance from God to mankind revealed through His Prophets, whose hearts and souls were in tune with God and who were the only ones who knew what messages they had received from God. There is no **authentic recording by earlier Prophets.** They were often transmitted by word of mouth, sometimes for hundreds of years. If they were recorded, in later years, they were **repeatedly altered by those seeking privilege** for political, social, and personal reasons (Ref. 12-p4). Consequently, most Holy Scriptures have monumental errors except the Quran, which remains in its original form.

The Holy Quran

The Quran is the collection of all revealed messages from God to **Mohammad (P).** Although unlettered (could not read or write), **he dictated all the messages** he received from God. Thousands of people memorized the entire Quran during the life of the Prophet (P). The Quran is the **only** Holy Scripture that is memorized by millions of people (called Hafez) even today.

1. Within two years of the Prophet's death, under order of Caliph Abu Bakr, Zaid bin Thabit, the Prophet's principal scribe, collected all the manuscripts, verified them and **wrote them down in book form.** Othman, the third Caliph, made many copies from the original, denoting correct recitation signs, and then sent them to the different regions of the countries under Muslim administration (Bukhari, V6 477-479). **Some of those original copies still exist; one in Tashkent, Uzbekistan and one in Topkapi, Istanbul, Turkey** (Ref. 37-p35). Today's Quran, word for word, is an exact copy of the original (Ref. 12 - pl 30 -131).

2. Dr. Maurice Bucaille, a French Christian physician, compared all scientific facts referred in Bible and Quran. He found many more scientific verses in the Quran. Each one of them is correct. He writes: "Whereas monumental **error are to be found in the Bible, I could not find a single error in the Quran"** (Ref. 12-p120).

3. **How on earth was it possible for an unlettered person to reveal the scientific mysteries 1,000 years ahead when no man on earth had any knowledge of them?**

What Every Woman Should Know   **19**

4. In the Quran, the highest honor of women is given to **Mary**: "O Mary, God has chosen you and purified you, chosen you above the women of all nations" (Quran 3:42). Out of 66 books of the Protestants and 73 of the Roman Catholics, not one is named after Mary or her son though you can find books named after Matthew, Mark, Luke, John, Paul, etc. If Mohammad (P) would be the author of Quran, he would have given this honor to his _own_ mother, beloved wife, or dearest daughter, not to Mary.

The Holy Bible

In the New Testament: four of the books are known as Gospels. Fourteen of the remaining books are attributed to Apostle St. Paul, four to Apostle John, two to Apostle Peter, one to each of James, Jude and Luke. The Catholic Version has 34 books. The Protestants do not consider these extra seven books to be authentic (Ref. 10-p 101). The books and letters that were dropped from the Bible in the 16h century were ordained by God but selected by **men**.

1. The Bible contains the messages from many great Prophets of the past. Unfortunately, the **Prophets did not record the messages** at the time of revelation. They were passed on by **oral transmission for generations,** sometimes for hundreds of years, before being written down (Ref. 12:p4-7). The Bible warns: "Prove all things; hold fast that which is good" (1 Thessalonians 5:21).

2. **50,000 Errors in the Bible:** This 1957 article appeared in the 'Christian Awake magazine' (ref. 11). Christians admit errors in the Bible, but in the conclusion the article maintains that it is still the authentic word of God. How so? Tischendorf uncovered over 14,800 "corrections" to the manuscript by nine (some say ten) separate "correctors," which had been applied to this one manuscript over a period from 400AD to 1200AD. Centuries of "correction" to the Bible in order to promote chosen doctrines has led to side-effects, some Christian scholars acknowledge that "errors" actually number over 48,000-50,000 errors.

3. **Authenticity:** Jesus (P) did not write or dictate the New Testament, nor was it written during his lifetime. The four **Gospels were written** some **35 to 85 years after Jesus (P) had left** this earth. After so many years, how is it possible to remember, word for word, what he had said earlier? Ecumenical translation of the Bible says: "...the evangelists...have collected and recorded in writing the material given to them by the oral tradition". (Ref. 12:p56).

4. **Authors of Holy Bible:** All knowledgeable Bible experts agree that the **true identities** of the authors of the Bible are **not known** (Ref. 12-p60, 63, 67& 69). St. Luke admits that <u>he is not the author of his Gospel</u> ("they delivered them to us" - Luke 1:2-3). Apostle Matthew cannot be the author of this Gospel. Instead of writing, "Jesus (P) saw me and asked me to follow him", it says: "he (Jesus (P)) saw a man called Matthew sitting at the tax office; and he said to him, 'Follow me'. And he rose and followed him"(Matthew. 9:9). Further, Matthew heavily copied from Mark who was not an eyewitness. Apostle John is not the author of the Gospel, which is named after him. Instead, several other authors wrote the Gospel of John (Ref. 12-p 69). The author of 'Samuel' is 'unknown', that of 'Chronicles' is 'unknown', probably collected and edited by Ezra!

- **Prophets Committed Sins Mentioned in the Holy Bible!** Prophets are special people chosen by God. They represent God on earth, and give guidance to mankind. It is <u>unthinkable</u> to see how prophets committed such sins mentioned in the Bible:

  - ➤ **Prophet Solomon worshipped false Gods in his old age. (**1 Kings 1:9-10).

  - ➤ **Solomon had 700 wives and 300 concubines;** and his wives turned his heart after other Gods...the Goddess of the Sido'nians (1 King 11:3).

  - ➤ **Prophet David danced naked before the people and before the Lord.** (2 Samuel 6:20).

  - ➤ **Prophet David** sent for Uriah's (neighbor) wife, Bathseba, and **committed adultery** with her, murdered her husband and married her. (2 Samuel 11:3-5).

  - ➤ **David's son Absalom committed incest with his father's concubines.** "Absalom went into his father's concubines in the sight of all Israel" (II Samuel 16:22).

  - ➤ **Prophet Noah was a drunk**, and lay uncovered in his tent and his son Ham saw the nakedness. (Genesis 9:21).

  - ➤ **"And Samson went to Gaza, and there he saw a harlot (prostitute), and he went into her."** (Judge 16:1)

  - ➤ **The spirit of God came upon Samson, who killed 30 men.** (Judge 14:19).

  - ➤ **Prophet Judah, the father of Jewish race, committed incest with his daughter-in-law Tamar:** "she is with child by harlotry." (Genesis 38:15-18).

- ➢ **The two daughters of Prophet Lot committed incest with their father.** Both daughters of Lot were with child by their father. (Genesis 19:32-36).

- ➢ **David's son Amnon committed rape and incest with his half-sister Tamar:** "and being stronger than she (Tamar), he (Amnon) forced her, and lay with her". (2 Samuel 13:1).

- ➢ **Prophet Aaron fashioned an idol** (the golden calf) for the Jews to worship (Exodus 32:1-4)

- ➢ **Rueben the son of Jacob (P) lay with Bilhah, his father's concubine.** (Genesis 35:22).

- • **Sex Literature in the Bible!** It is difficult to believe the immoralities written in God's revealed book, the Bible!

- ➢ Women's breasts in the Bible. (Songs 1:13, 3:1).

- ➢ Songs of Solomon -book of sexual description (Songs 4.1, 8.8)

- ➢ Sexual descriptions. (Proverb 7:7).

- ➢ The Sexual language in Ezekiel. (Ezekiel 16:1, 26, 33)

- ➢ Story of two prostitutes-Aho'lah & A-hol-I-bah (Ezekiel 23:2)

- ➢ God makes people fall into adultery. (Amos 7:16, Isiah 3:16, Jeremiah 13:22, Nah 3:4, Hos 2:2).

- ➢ Disgusting commands to Ezekiel. (Ezekiel 4:12).

- ➢ Eating dung and drinking 'piss'. (2 King 18:27).

- ➢ "A bastard should not enter into the congregation of the Lord." (Deut. 23:2); "They are bastards, and not sons." (Hebrew 12:8)

- ➢ "Rescue her husband". (Duet. 25:11).

- ➢ Biblical expressions. (Eccl. 3:1, 7:1, Job 35:10, 1. Sam. 2:1).

- • **Holy Bible on Slavery**
  - ➢ **"...you may buy male and female slaves** from among the nations that are round about you" (Leviticus 25:44)

  - ➢ "...You may bequeath them to your sons after you, to **inherit as a possession forever"** (Leviticus 25:46).

  - ➢ "When you buy **a Hebrew slave, he shall serve six years,** and in the seventh he shall go out free, for nothing" (Exodus 21:2).

  - ➢ Prophet Noah gets drunk himself and curses grandson **Canaan** to **slavery for no fault of his own!** (Genesis 6:10).

- • **Holy Bible On Alcohol**

- ➤ "Give strong drink unto him that is ready to perish, and wine unto those that be of heavy hearts. **Let him drink,** and forget his poverty, and **remember his misery no more"** (Proverb 31:6-7).

- ➤ "Drink no longer water, but use a little wine for your stomach's sake..." (1 Timothy 5:23).

- ➤ Jesus (P) said to his mother Mary: "**Woman, what have I to do with thee?** Mine hour is not yet come" (John 2:3-4).

- **Paul and Racism**: Paul said: "We ourselves, who are Jews by birth and not Gentile sinners." (Galatians 2:15). "Cast out the slave and her son, for the son of slave shall not inherit with the son of the free woman. So brethren we are not children of the slave but of the free woman." (Galatians 4:22).

- **Gentiles in the Bible**: Lord said: "Behold I will lift up my hand to the gentiles, and raise up my signal to the people, and they shall bring your sons in their bosom, and your daughters shall be carried on their shoulders. Kings shall be your foster fathers, and their queens your nursing mothers. With their faces to the ground they shall bow down to you, and lick the dust of your feet." (Isiah 49:22). "Lift up your eyes round about, and see, they all gather together, they come to you. The wealth of the nations" (KJV: "gentiles shall come unto you and the sons of the foreigners shall build up your walls, and their kings shall minister unto you. For the nation and kingdom that will not serve you shall perish; those nations shall be utterly laid waste. You shall suck the milk of the nations. You shall suck the breast of kings." (Isiah 60:4). "And strangers shall stand and feed your flocks, and the sons of the alien shall be your plowmen and your vinedressers. But you shall be named the priests of the lord. Men shall call you the ministers of God. You shall eat the riches of the nations." KJV "Gentiles and in their glory shall you boast yourselves." (Isiah 61:5).

- **Only 144,000 Zionists Redeemed and Taken to Heaven**: "On mount Zion stood the lamb, and with him a 144,000 who had his name and his father's name written on their foreheads. They sing a new song before the throne...no one could learn that song except the 144,000 who had been redeemed from the earth. It is those who have not defiled themselves with women, for they are chaste. It is these who follow the lamb wherever he goes; these have been redeemed from mankind as first fruits of God and the Lamb." (This contradicts redemption of Jesus to all mankind, and deprives some prophets from joining these 144,000 Zionists, like David, Lot,

Judah, whom the Bible referred to them cases of adultery with their own daughters, daughters-in-law, and their neighbors) (Rev. 14:1).

- **Kill Women, Children, Animals**: Lord said: "Go through the city, and smite: let not your eye spare, neither have you pity. Slay utterly old and young, both maids and little children, and women." (Ezek. 9:5). Lord said unto Moses: "Avenge the children of the Mid'-an'ites. They warred against the Mid'-an'ites, as the Lord commanded Moses, and they slay all the males. And they took all women as captives, and their little ones, and took the spoil of all their cattle, and all their flocks, and all their goods. And they burnt all their cities wherein they dwelt, and all their goodly castles, with fire." (Numbers 31:1). Moses said: "Have you saved all the women alive? Now kill every male among the little ones, and kill every woman that has known a man by lying with him, but all the young girls who have not known a man by lying with him keep alive for yourselves." Joshua said to the people of Israel: "The Lord has given you the city (of the Canaanites)... all silver, and gold, and vessels of brass and iron, are consecrated unto the Lord: They shall come into the treasury of the Lord. The people utterly destroyed all that was in the city, both man and woman, young and old, and ox and sheep, and ass, with the edge of the sword." (Joshua 6:16).

- **Kill, Kidnap, And Enslave**: "So the Canaanites have dwelt in the midst of E'phraim to this day, but have become slaves to do forced labor." (Joshua 16:10, 17:13, Judge 1:30). The congrega- tion of Benjamin sent 12,000 of their bravest men, and commanded them: "Go and smite the inhabitants of Ja'-besh-gil'ead with the edge of the sword; also the women and the little ones. Every male and every woman that has laid with a male you shall utterly destroy." (Judge 21:10). "And they found among the inhabitants' 400 young virgins who had not known a man by lying with him; and they brought them to the camp of Shiloh, which is the land of Canaan. And Benjamin returned at that time, and they gave them the women whom they had saved alive of the women of Ja'besh-gil'ead, but they did not suffice for them."

- **Steal Women**: They commanded Benjaminites, saying: "Go and lie in wait in the vineyard, and watch, if the daughters of Shiloh go out to dance in the dances, then come out of the vineyard and seize each man his wife from daughters of Shiloh. The Benjaminites did so, and took their wives from dancers whom they caught."

- **Kill and Take Their Properties**: "When you draw near to a city to fight against it, offer terms of peace to it. And if its answer to you in peace and it opens to you, then all the people who are found in it shall be forced labor for you and shall serve you. But if it makes no peace with you, then you shall besiege it. You shall put all its males to the sword, but the women and the little ones, the cattle and every thing else all its spoil, you shall take as booty for yourselves; and... spoil of your enemies. (Deuteronomy 20:10)

- **Revenge, Sword, Fire**: "Our God is destroying fire." (Hebrew 12:29). "O Lord, you God of Vengeance." (Psalms 94:1). "Why do not you pardon my transgression and take away my iniquity?" (Job 7:21). God said: "You have feared the sword, the sword I will bring upon you." (Ezekiel 11:8). "I will slay that left of them with the sword, not one of them shall flee away. I will command the sword, and it shall slay them. "(Amos 9:1). "I will send the sword after them, until I have consumed them." (Jeremiah 49:37). <u>Those who say Islam is the religion of the sword should know that the word "sword" is **NEVER** mentioned in Quran while the Bible mentions it many times, in the way that you see here.</u> "I will unsheathe the sword after them. I will let a few of them escape sword, from famine and pestilence." (Ezekiel 12:14).

- **Bible Misrepresents God's Mercy**: The Lord said: "I will make them eat the flesh of their sons and their daughters, and every one shall eat the flesh of his neighbor." (Jerem. 19:7). "If you will not hearken to me.. I will bring a sword upon you...you shall eat the flesh of your sons and daughters." (Levi. 26:14). "Look O Lord, and see! With whom you have done that: should women eat their fruit and children of a span long? The hands of compassionate women have boiled their own children, they became their food." (Lament 2:20).

- **Sword & Fire in New Testament**: Jesus (P) said: "Do you not think that I have come to make peace on earth? I have not come to bring peace, but a sword. For I have come to set a man against his father, and a daughter against her mother." (Matthew 10:34). Jesus (P) said: "I came to cast fire upon the earth, and would that it was already kindled. Do you think that I have come to give peace on earth? No, I tell you, but rather division; for from henceforth in one house there will be five divided three against two, and two against three. They will be divided, father against son, and son against father, mother against daughter, and daughter against her mother." (Luke 12:49). "For these enemies of mine, who did not want me to reign over them, bring them here and slay them before me." (Luke 19:27). "If any one comes to me and does not HATE his own father and mother and wife, and children, and brothers and sisters, yes and even his own life: he cannot be my disciple." (Luke 14:26)

- **Jesus (P) With His Mother**: He said to Mary: "Woman, what have I to do with you." (John. 2:4). Then one said unto Jesus (P): "Behold, your mother and brethren stand without, desiring to talk to you but he answered and said: Who is my mother? And who are my brethren?" (Matthew 12:47).

- **Mothers Eat Their Children:** "Look O Lord…Women are eating the bodies of their children they loved."(Lament 2:20). "My hope in the lord is gone." (According to the Good News Bible) "We have sinned and rebelled, and you O Lord have not forgiven us. You pursued us and killed, your mercy was hidden by your anger. Slaying without pity, you have wrapped yourself with a cloud so that no prayer can pass through." (Lament 3:18). "The tongue of the nursling cleaves to the roof of its mouth for thirst, the children beg for food. Their visage is blacker than soot. Their skin has shriveled upon their bones. The hands of the compassionate women have boiled their own children. They became their food in the destruction of the daughter of my people. The Lord gave full vent to his wrath, and poured out his hot anger, and he kindled a fire in Zion." (Lament 4:4)

- **David Dances Naked Before God**: "And David and all the houses of Israel played before the Lord of all manner of instruments made of fir wood, even on harps, and on psalteries, and on tumbrels. And David danced before the lord with all his might." (2 Samuel 6:5). "So David and all the house of Israel brought up the ark of the Lord with shouting, and with the sound of the trumpet. When Michele Saul's daughter looked through a window, and saw king David leaping and dancing before the Lord she despised him in her heart.. And said, "How glorious was the king of Israel today who Uncovered himself today in the eyes of the hand maid of his servant, as one of the vain fellows shamelessly uncovered himself?" David said, "it was before the Lord, which chose me before your father... Therefore will I play before the Lord."

- Even though St. Paul directly contradicted what Jesus (P) had said and practiced, the majority of his books are included in the New Testament. It is of interest to note that one of St. Paul's companions was Luke and St. Paul was missing for a few years when Mark's Gospel was written. Further St. Paul "was considered to be a traitor to Jesus (P)' thoughts by the latter's family and by the Apostles who had stayed in Jerusalem" (Ref. 12, p 52 & p 67).

5. There are innumerable contradictions and errors in the Bible. The Bible itself recognized the **lack of it's authenticity** by this verse: "How can you, say, 'We are wise, and the law of the Lord is with us'? **But behold, the false pen of the scribes has made it into a lie"** (Jeremiah 8:8). Most biblical scholars estimate around 50,000 mistakes/contradictions in the New Testament alone. (www.geocities.com/tltac/ch4.html).

The Holy Book Torah

The Jews believe their Old Testament (OT) to be faultless words of Moses and the prophets. The "OT" is made up of the "**Torah**", (also called the "**Pentateuch**"), and the "books of the prophets". The "Torah" consists of the first five books of the OT: "**Genesis**", "**Exodus**", "**Leviticus**", "**Numbers**", and "**Deuteronomy**". After the Christians decided to incorporate the OT into their Bible, they began to study these books in great detail.

1. When someone wanted to know what happened in the past, they would go back and study the OT to find the answer. People found various passages on the <u>same topic</u>; conflicting accounts of many matters. For instance, in the 11th century, it was noticed that the list of Edomite kings in Genesis 36 names kings who lived long after Moses was dead. Then people also began to see statements such as "to this day" something is true. Deuteronomy says: "These are the words that Moses spoke to the children of Israel across Jordan..". <u>But Moses (author) himself never was in Israel in his life!</u>

2. Deuteronomy 34:5-10 explains how Moses died and where he was buried. **How is this possible?** The explanation of these verses are that these were written by Moses, but later prophets, as well as "inspired" scribes had added a couple of lines here and there. In this manner the text remained 100% the "inspiration" of God. This explanation **does not** stand up to scrutiny because the style and literary characteristics of the verses are the same throughout.

3. **The doublets:** Later, the trend became to explain any and all discrepancies through abstracts and elaborate interpretations, or through additional narrative details that did not appear in the biblical text. Around this time, a startling new discovery was made. It was noticed that the stories in the five books of Moses were made up of **doublets**. A doublet is a case of one story being told twice. Even in the English translation of the Bible, the doublets are noticeable. These doublets have been masterfully intertwined so that they become one

narrative. For example, there are doublets of the creation of the world, the covenant between God and Abraham (P), the naming of Isaac, Abraham (P)'s claim that his wife Sarah was his sister, the story of Jacob (P)'s journey to Mesopotamia, Jacob (P)'s revelation at Beth-El,...and on and on. In many cases these doublets actually contradict one another. The doublets were claimed to be complementary, not contradictive, and were meant to teach lessons by their "apparent" contradiction. Later, when the doublets were separated into two separate accounts, each account was always consistent about the name of the deity that it used. One would refer to God as Yahweh/Jehovah. The other always referred to Him as Elohim (God). Other literary characteristics were found to be common to one group or the other. It was obvious that someone had taken two separate accounts, cut them up, and then woven them together quite masterfully so that their actions would not be discovered until many centuries later.

4. Professor Richard Friedman of the University of California, San Diego, earned his Doctorate in Hebrew Bible at Harvard University. He is one of many scholars who attempted to critically study these "source" documents of the "five books of Moses" in order to arrive at the identity of the authors, the time period when each was written, the motives for writing each narrative, and other information. In his book "Who Wrote the Bible?", Prof. Friedman presents strong evidence that each "source document" was written by a person or persons who, while on the surface seem to narrate the same stories, in actuality had distinctly different goals they wished to achieve. Each source emphasizes a certain branch of the Jews, their nobility, birthright, and closeness to God. He also shows how in one version, Joseph is saved by his brother Ruben (the firstborn of Israel), while in another version it is Judah who saves him. The author presents countless other proofs of these claims.

5. The remaining books of the OT were known to have been preserved from change and truly to be the words of the claimed authors. Grolier's encyclopedia says: "...Joshua tells of a thorough conquest of Canaan, but Judges contains traditions of the Hebrew tribes in the period before the monarchy that reveal the conquest as partial. The books of Samuel are about the founding of the monarchy under Saul and David and contain a magnificent early source for the life of David, probably written about 961-22 BC.

6. Fourteen hundred years ago, back when it was a blasphemy of the highest order punishable by death to dare allege that the claimed authors of the Bible were not the true authors, e.g. that Moses did not write the "books of Moses", the Quran was sent down to Mohammad

(P) by God with the claim that "the people of the Book" (Jews and Christians) had changed the book of God. Mohammad (P) further claimed that he was sent with true religion of God, which was sent down upon Moses and Jesus as well.

The books of the Christians: Christian scholars today call the Gospels of Matthew, Mark, and Luke, the "Synoptic" (One eyed) Gospels. They all seem to have had access to a common source document they were working from when they wrote their Gospels. Now they are beginning to recognize that the alleged authors are not the true authors. Similarly, countless verses of the Gospel of John, as well as other historical discrepancies, show that John did not write the Gospel of John. Some scholars are now beginning to suspect that 'One Source' may indeed be the Gospel of Barnabas. It is much larger than the others, by all measures it is an authentic Gospel, and it contains all of the stories contained in these three Gospels without the contradictions found therein. "Then woe to those who write the book (of God) with their own hands and then say: 'This is from God'..." (Quran 2:79).

The Holy Book Talmud

The Talmud is Judaism's holiest book. Its authority takes precedence over the Old Testament. The Jewish Scribes claim that the Talmud is partly a collection of traditions Moses gave them in oral form. Christ condemned the traditions of the Mishnah (early Talmud) and those who taught it (scribes and Pharisees), because the Talmud nullifies the teachings of the Holy Bible:"...teaching for doctrines the commandments of men. For laying aside the commandment of God..."(Mark, Chapter 7, King James Bible). The Judeo-Christian notion is that the Old Testament is the supreme book of Judaism. But this is not so. The Pharisees teach doctrine of the commandments of rabbis, **not God**. There are two versions: the Jerusalem Talmud and the Babylonian Talmud. The Babylonian Talmud is regarded as the authoritative version. Some teachings of the **Babylonian Talmud**:

1. If a heathen (gentile) hits a Jew, the gentile must be killed. (Sanhedrin 58b)

2. A Jew need not pay a gentile the wages owed him for work. (Sanhedrin 57a)

3. If an ox of an Israelite gores an ox of a Canaanite there is no liability; but if an ox of a Canaanite gores an ox of an Israelite...the payment is to be in full. (Baba Kamma 37b)

4. If a Jew finds an object lost by a gentile it does not have to be returned. (Baba Mezia 24a)

5. God will not spare a Jew who "marries his daughter to an old man or takes a wife for his infant son or returns a lost article to a Cuthean..." (Sanhedrin 76a)

6. When a Jew murders a gentile, there will be no death penalty. What a Jew steals from a gentile he may keep. (Sanhedrin 57a)

7. The gentiles are outside the protection of the law and God has "exposed their money to Israel." (Baba Kamma 37b)

8. Jews may use lies (subterfuges) to circumvent (mislead) a Gentile. (Baba Kamma 113a)

9. All gentile children are animals. (Yebamoth 98a)

10. Gentile girls are in a state of niddah (filth) from birth. (Abodah Zarah 36b)

11. Gentiles prefer sex with cows. (Abodah Zarah 22a-22b)

12. She (Miriam) who was the descendant of princes and governors played the harlot with carpenters. (Sanhedrin 106a). Also in footnote #2 to Shabbath 104b of the Soncino edition, it is stated that in the "uncensored" text of the Talmud it is written that Jesus (P)' mother, "Miriam the hairdresser," had sex with many men.

13. "Hast thou heard how old Balaam (Jesus (P)) was? --He replied: It is not actually stated but since it is written, Bloody and deceitful men shall not live out half their days"-- it follows that he was 33 or 34 years old. (Sanhedrin 106).

14. Jesus (P) is in hell, being boiled in hot excrement. (Gittin 57a)

15. It is taught that on the eve of Passover, Jesus (P) was hung, and forty days before this the proclamation was made: "Jesus (P) is to be stoned to death because he has practiced sorcery and has lured the people to idolatry...He was an enticer and of such thou shall not pity or condone." (Sanhedrin 43a)

16. Jesus (P) was executed by a proper rabbinical court for idolatry, inciting other Jews to idolatry, and contempt of rabbinical authority. All classical Jewish sources that mention his execution are quite happy to take responsibility for it.

17. The more popular accounts--which were nevertheless taken quite seriously-- in addition to the above crimes, they accuse him of witchcraft. The very name 'Jesus (P)' was for Jews a symbol of all that is abominable and this popular tradition still persists.

18. The Hebrew form of the name Jesus (P)/Yeshu--was interpreted as an acronym for the curse, 'may his name and memory be wiped out,' which is used as an extreme form of abuse. Anti-Zionist Orthodox Jews sometimes refer to Herzl as 'Herzl Jesus (P)' and I have found in religious Zionist writings expressions such as "Nasser Jesus (P)" and more recently 'Arafat Jesus (P)" (Dr. Israel Shahak, Jewish History, Jewish Religion, p.97- 98, 118).

19. Christians and others who reject the Talmud will go to hell and be punished there for all generations. (Rosh Hashanah 17a)

20. Those who read the New Testament will have no portion in the world to come. (Sanhedrin 90a)

21. Adam had sexual intercourse with all the animals in the Garden of Eden. (Yebamoth 63a)

22. A woman who had intercourse with a beast is eligible to marry a Jewish priest. A woman who has sex with a demon is also eligible to marry a Jewish priest. (Yebamoth 59b)

23. No rabbi can ever go to hell. (Hagigah 27a)

24. A rabbi debates God and defeats Him. God admits the rabbi won the debate. (Baba Mezia 59b)

25. It is forbidden for dogs, women or palm trees to pass between two men, or any others to walk between dogs, women or palm trees. Special dangers are involved if the women are menstruating or sitting at a crossroads. (Pesahim 111a)

26. A Jewish man is obligated to say this prayer every day: "Thank you God for not making me a gentile, a woman or a slave." (Menahoth 43b-44a)

27. Minor Tractates. Soferim 15, Rule 10. This is the saying of Rabbi Simon ben Yohai: *Tob shebe goyyim harog* (Even the best of the gentiles should all be killed). This is from the original Babylonian Talmud as quoted by the 1907 Jewish Encyclopedia, published by Funk and Wagnalls and compiled by Isidore Singer, under the entry, "Gentile," (p.617). The original Talmud passage has been concealed in translation. In today's context, Israelis annually take part in a pilgrimage to the grave of Simon ben Yohai, to honor this rabbi who advocated the extermination of non-Jews. (Jewish Press, June 9, 1989, p. 56B). For example: On Purim, Feb. 25, 1994, Israeli army officer Baruch Goldstein, an orthodox Jew from Brooklyn, massacred 40 Palestinian civilians, including children, while they knelt in prayer at Abraham (P)'s mosque in Hebron. Goldstein was

a disciple of the late Brooklyn Rabbi Meir Kahane, who told CBS News about his teaching that Arabs are "<u>dogs</u>" as derived "from Talmud." (CBS 60 Minutes, "Kahane").

28. University of Jerusalem Professor Ehud Sprinzak described Kahane and Goldstein's philosophy: "They believe it's God's will that they commit violence against goyim, a Hebrew term for non-Jews." (NY Daily News, Feb. 26, 1994, p.5). Rabbi Yaacov Perrin said: "One million Arabs are **not worth even a Jewish fingernail**." (NY Daily News, Feb. 28, 1994, p.6).

The Jewish Talmudic book Sanhedrin states...

1. Jesus was stoned and then "hanged" (crucified) (Sanh. 43a-45b)

2. Jesus' apostles were all killed (Sanh. 43a-b)

3. Jesus was crucified as a blasphemer (Sanh. 46a)

4. Jesus was burned after he was lowered into dung to his armpits with his mouth forced open and molten lead was poured in, burning his internal organs. (Sanh. 52a)

5. Jesus was strangled after being lowered into the dung (Sanh. 56a, 106b)

6. Jesus is in Hell where his punishment is boiling in hot semen. (Gitten 57A)

7. Jesus committed bestiality, corrupted the people, and is turned into Hell. (Sanh. 105a)

8. Jesus limped on one foot, was blind in one eye, practiced enhancement by way of membrum, committed bestiality with an ass, and was a fool who did not know his beast's mind. (Sanh. 105a, 105b)

9. Jesus attempted to seduce a woman, was excommunicated by a Rabbi, and then worshipped a brick. He was a seducer of Israel and practiced magic. (Sanh. 107b)

10. Jesus is the chief repository of the criminal law of the Talmud. (Sanhedrin index) (Dilling p. 51)

Talmudic Doctrine: Non-Jews are NOT human

1. The Talmud specifically defines all who are not Jews as non-human animals, and dehumanizes gentiles as not descendants of Adam.

2. "...Simon ben Yohai states, "you are called men (Adam) but the idolaters are not called men (Adam)." (Yebamoth 61a)

3. The Mosaic Law states that touching a human corpse or grave imparts uncleanness to those who touch it.

Moses Maimonides: Advocate of Extermination

Moses Maimonides is considered the greatest codifier and philosopher in Jewish history. He is often referred to as 'Rambam', after his initials, Rabenu Moshe Ben Maimon. "Our Rabbi, Moses son of Maimon." (Maimonides' Principles, edited by Aryeh Kaplan, Union of Orthodox Jewish Congregations of America, p.3).

Maimonides taught the followings principles:

1. If we see an idolater (gentile) being swept away or drowning in the river, we should not help him. If we see that his life is in danger, we should not save him. (Maimonides, Mishnah Torah, (Moznaim Publishing, Brooklyn, NY, 1990, Ch.10, English Trans.), p.184)

2. "It is a mitzvah (religious duty) to eradicate Jewish traitors, minnim, and apikorsim, and to cause them to descend to the pit of destruction, since they cause difficulty to the Jews and sway the people away from God, as did Jesus (P) of Nazareth and his students, and Tzadok, Baithos, and their students. May the name of the wicked rot!" (Maimonides, Mishnah Torah, (Chapter 10), p.184). The preceding statement states that Jesus (P) was an example of a min (plural: minnim). The commentary also states that the students of Tzadok were defined as those Jews who deny the truth of the Talmud and who uphold only the written law (i.e. the Old Testament).

3. Maimonides "spent 12 years extracting every decision and law from the Talmud, and arranging them all into 14 systematic volumes. The work was finally completed in 1180, and was called Mishnah Torah, or 'Code of the Torah.'"

Hinduism

Hindus are divided into thousands of communities and tribes, each having its own religious beliefs, rituals, modes of worship, etc. Hinduism is not a revealed religion and, therefore, has neither a founder nor definite teachings; no common system of doctrines.

1. <u>Polytheism</u>: Hindus believe in many gods and goddesses. Some of them are human (e.g. Krishna, Rama), some animals (e.g. fish, monkey, rat, snake), some animal-humans (as in the case of Ganesh, who has the head of an elephant with trunk and the body of a human), and some others are natural phenomena (dawn, fire, sun).

2. **Krishna:** The Indian god Krishna bears a tremendous resemblance to Jesus. He was the incarnation of the supreme god Vishnu in the womb of Devaki. He was born in a cave. His foster father was told to flee and hide him lest king Kansa might take his life. King Kansa had ordered all male infants born on that night to be slain. One of his first miracles was the healing of a leper. He was later slain and this resulted in an eclipse of the sun and a black circle around the moon. Spirits were seen on all sides and he descended into hell, rose again, and ascended into heaven. He will have a "second coming" in the future, which his followers continually await. There are countless other similarities with what is known today as "Christianity" even though Hinduism was well establish centuries before the birth of Jesus. Krishna is regarded as a great hero; it was not until about the 4th century BC that he was elevated to the position of a god.

3. **Superiority of the Brahman:** The Brahmans occupy highest position in the hierarchy of the caste system (discussed later). They are said to have sprung from the mouth of Brahma (God); they are the rightful possessors of the Veda. They possess spiritual superiority by birth. They have the monopolistic right to act as priests, conduct religious ceremonies and festivals, and accept alms. The Brahman is the deity on earth by his divine status, "born to fulfill dharma". Whatever exists in the world is his property. On account of the excellence of his origin, he is entitled to all.

4. **Authority of the Veda:** Veda is recognized as absolute authority in Hinduism, but the low-caste Hindus have no access to the scripture because they are considered impure by birth. The only people who are allowed to read and listen to the scripture are the Brahmans, the sole custodians of the Veda, hardly benefit from it as well because it is written in Sanskrit. Its content has long been practically <u>unknown</u> to most Hindus, and it is seldom drawn upon for literal advice.

5. **Who are the Brahmins?** The word 'Brahmin' incorporates all the upper-caste Hindus of India. They claim that they were made from God Brahma's head; they are chosen people of God. Worshipping a Brahmin is akin to worshipping God incarnate. Serving a Brahmin and offering him alms is like serving God himself. As a result, 5% of the Indian population has psychologically enslaved the other 95%. The Brahmins are the "Aryans", invaders of India, who entered the country thousands of years ago via the Khyber Pass. Over the centuries they have established themselves firmly on Indian soil by ruling over, and enslaving, the country's original inhabitants.

6. **Divisions Among the Brahmins:** In Southern India the main divisions among Brahmins are the Ayyars and the Ayyangers. These two groups have their gods, writings, families, culture and above all, the century-old concealed rivalry between them for power and influence. The Ayyars are, by physical composition, more direct descendants of the Aryans invaders. They have fair complexions, long noses and other physical characteristics of Germans.

7. **Caste System:** Hindu society is divided into several thousands of castes and sub-castes and keeps nearly 95% of the Hindus in perpetual disgrace and permanently condemned to an inferior social status. There is no Hindu without a caste who is bound by caste from birth to death, who becomes subject to social regulation and tradition of the caste over which he has no control. A person born in a caste carries the name of that caste as a part of his surname. Caste differences find their expression largely in connection with marriages and eating together. Castes are not equal in status but arranged in a vertical order in which one caste is at the top and is the highest (the Brahman), another at the bottom and is the lowest (the Dalit) and in between them there are the Kshatriya, the Vashya and the Sudra in a descending order. This inequality in status is said to be an outcome of a person's deeds (good or bad) accomplished in his previous life. The great distinctions of caste are to be maintained not only in the earthly life, but also after death. According to Purana, after death, the virtuous Brahman goes to the abode of Brahma, the good Khatriya to that of Indra, the worthy Vashya to that of the Maruts, and the dutiful Sudra to that of the Gandharvas. The Untouchable (Dalit) **does not deserve any place in any heaven**.

8. **Origin of the Caste System:** 'Caste' is a Portuguese word, used by the Portuguese as equivalent of 'varna' (means 'color'). Caste originally was a color-bar, in India, and later in America, served at first to separate free men from slaves. When the fair-skinned Aryans (foreign conquerors) invaded India, about 2,000 years before Jesus

Christ, they defeated the dark-skinned local indigenous people, Dravidians. The Aryans subjugated them, learned many things from them, and built up the Hindu Civilization. Aryans created the caste system, and thereby excluded the locals from their own society with the name of Sudra (means slave). When the ancient priests set themselves up as an exclusive caste of Brahmans in order to establish their self-assumed superiority, they had to inflict degradation on all other Hindus (original Indians) and press them down to various layers of subordination. They had to keep people divided, disunited, weak, degraded, to deny them learning, refinement and opportunities of advancement, and permanently and unalterably to tie them down to a low status in society.

9. **Caste Determines Duty:** The basic duty of every individual is determined by his caste. The Brahman is the rightful possessor of the Veda and is the chief of the whole creation. He has the exclusive right to become a priest. The Khatriya is described as the dispenser of justice, to punish law-breakers; he exercises the civil power and to his tender mercies the Brahmans could hand over law-breakers. He has to see that the various castes attend to their prescribed duties; but in doing this work he must abide by the decisions of the Brahmans. The Vashya comprises the merchant, the agriculturist, and the keeper of cattle (his chief work). The Sudra has been created to serve the other three castes (i.e., the fair-skinned Aryans). "He is spoken of as a slave, his property, as well as his person, being at the disposal of his master." The Untouchable (Dalit) is to perform the most unpleasant tasks: cleaning lavatories, carrying night soil, skinning carcasses and making footwear.

Hindu Pundit (scholar) Suggests Hindus to Embrace Islam

A book titled 'Kalki Otar' written by ved Prakash, a Hindu Pundit, holding a high position in Allahabad University, published in India, disclosed that according to the holy books of the Hindu religion, Kalki Otar was to be born in Arab islands, his father's name would be 'vishno Bhagat' and mother's name would be 'Somanb' and both the words are Sansikarised version of 'Abdullah' and 'Amenah'. The book said that he was to get knowledge through an angel in a cave, and this has already happened in the life of Mohammad (P). Therefore, Hindus should embrace Islam immediately. Mr. Prakash presented his research before 8 Indian grand pundits and they all endorsed his research in 18 May 1999.

The Quran testifies that God has sent prophets to every people. It is not surprising to find prophecies about the Last Prophet, Muhammad, in previously revealed scriptures, such as in Hindu Holy Scriptures.

Islam: the Final Religion

Religions, in general, are named after their founders. Christianity is named after Jesus **Christ**, Buddhism after Gotama **Buddha**, Marxism after Karl **Marx**, and Confucianism after **Confucius** and Zoroastrianism after **Zoroaster**. Judaism was named after the tribe of **Judah** and the country of **Jude**. But Islam was **not** named after any person, tribe, or country. Although many non-Muslims often refer to it (wrongly) as "Muhammadinism", it was named after the principle for which it stands. Religions can be divided into two broad groups, **philosophical and revealed religions**. The founders of the philosophical religions were highly respectable and intelligent people of their society. They never claimed to be Prophets or to have received revelations from God. The founders of the **revealed religions were Prophets** and they met the following **criteria of Prophethood** as laid down in the Holy Scriptures:

1. They received revelations from God or His angels in visions/dreams.

2. They made prophecies that came to pass.

3. Works of the Prophets endured.

4. Prophets had absolute trust in God even during the most difficult circumstances and God sustained them.

5. Prophets were warners to people about consequences of disobeying God's laws. They were also givers of glad tidings of God's kindness, mercy and forgiveness; and promised that the weak and the needy will be comforted.

Prophet Mohammad (P) meets all the above criteria and many non-Muslim scholars of the Holy Scriptures now recognize him as a Prophet. Prophets were special people who received revelations from God. For us to know them correctly, those messages must have been recorded meticulously at the time of revelation and then transmitted underlined. If we examine all the Holy Books of the revealed religions, **Mohammad (P) is the only Prophet who dictated each and every revelation he had received and even checked their accuracy.** Those revelations were complied into a book, which is known as the **Quran**. No one has altered one letter in that book. **Today the Quran is the only authentic revealed Holy Book in the world that remains *unaltered*.** Islam is the religion of this authentic unaltered Holy book. **The word 'Islam' means submission to the will and law of God.** The other meaning of the word is **peace (through God)**. One who willingly submits to the will and laws of God is a **Muslim**.

Islam is the universal religion for all mankind. Every creation in the universe submits to the law of God. Every cell of our body was created by the physical and chemical laws laid down by God. As such, by definition, all humans are born as Muslims as the Quran says. After attaining maturity, when we use our God-given intelligence to deny His existence or refuse to submit to His commandments, and instead follow family tradition, etc., we become non-Muslims. **All the Prophets of the past willingly submitted to the will of God.**

Five Pillars of Islam

Islam is traditionally explained under the headings of **"Five Pillars of Islam"** namely, (1) Faith/Iman, (2) Prayer or Salat, (3) Fasting or Swam, (4) Poor due or Zakat, and (5) Pilgrimage or Hajj. Faith is a set of beliefs and the remaining four are actions and practices reflecting these beliefs.

1. **'Iman' or Faith: Iman is the unshakable belief, without a shadow of doubt, in**

   ➤ **The existence of one and only true God. Faith in the existence of the ONE and ONLY true God:** Faith begins with God and all His absolute attributes. He is the **Sole Creator** of the universe. He has no beginning and no end. He is Eternal, Absolute and Everlasting. He is All-Powerful, All-Knowing, Self sufficient, and Self-Sustaining. He shares His absolute attributes with **no one**. **The only** *unforgivable* **sin is to associate any one with God's absolute attributes. (For example, assigning partners to Him).**

   ➤ **All the true Prophets of the past, and Mohammad (P) is the last Prophet. Faith in all the true Prophets of the past, and Mohammad (P) is the last Prophet:** Prophets were special people chosen by God. The Quran says that not one of them is to be distinguished above the rest (Quran 2:285). They were protected by God and were sinless, truthful, and righteous. The guidance from a Prophet assures guarantee of its truth. All **Prophets taught the same religion:** to recognize God the creator, to submit to His will and to obey Him. There will be life after death. The Prophets differed **only** in their method of teaching and the extent of God given worldly laws, which depended on the social development at the time they were here and their specific circumstances.

   ➤ **All the revealed unaltered Holy Books of God. Faith in all the revealed unaltered Holy Books of God:** Holy Books of revealed religions are a guidance from God. In the past the teachings of Prophets were either not recorded properly or later mixed up with false stories, legends, rituals, and man made laws. What we have today are not in the language of the Prophets. They are **translations**. They were addressed only to a specific group of people for a specific period of time. The only **exception** is the Quran. It was revealed in Arabic (since the inhabitants spoke Arabic—**not** because Arabs are superior, etc) and it is still in Arabic, its **original form**. The Quran is a guidance for the entire mankind till the last day.

➤ **The angels of God. Faith in the angels of God:** Angels are invisible creations of God. God conducts the affairs of the universe through them. They do not have any freedom of choice and are incapable of disobedience. In contrast to the angels, there is another invisible creation of God called Jinn. They are created from fire and have limited freedom of choice like humans. Satan belongs to them.

➤ **Life after death and the Day of Judgment. Faith in life after death and the Day of Judgment:** A very firm and unshakable belief in life after death and the Day of Judgment is the single most important factor that determines the behavior of a person in this life. This world will end, and then there will be resurrection of the dead, followed by the Day of Judgment. People will be rewarded, forgiven, or punished according to their activities in this world and will end up in either heaven or hell. **Only God knows precise time and date of end of this world.**

➤ **Divine Decree (Divine fate), whether good or evil. Divine Fate:** A very firm belief that everything in the universe that has happened in the past and that will happen in the future are within the knowledge of God and with His permission only. Whatever a person chooses, the results whether good or bad are within the knowledge of God and with His permission.

2. **Prayer or 'Salat':** Worship of God was ordained for all the people *as well as* Prophets of the past. The Islamic concept of worship deals with every aspect of life. All things that please God are good. **Any act that pleases God is a form of worship.** If you lead a truthful and righteous life according to the laws of God, help the poor, or feed the hungry **without the intention of personal worldly gain**, you are worshipping God. Besides these acts of worship, there are daily prayers performed five times a day at specific hours, according to the instructions given by Mohammad (P), facing towards the direction of Kaba in Mecca built by Abraham (P). The various positions and postures during the prayers are external expressions of one's submission to God. During prayer one seeks forgiveness, help and guidance from God directly. There is no intercessor between a believer and his Lord. Prayer strengthens the foundation of faith. **The**

prayer is five times a day; it helps keep one away from evil deeds and continually reminds one of God.

3. **Fasting or 'Swam':** In the past, Prophets and people used to fast, **Jesus (P) fasted for forty days** (Matthew 4:2). Fasting is obligatory for the Muslims during the month of Ramadhan, the 9th month of the lunar year. They refrain from all food, drink, and sex from before sunrise to after sunset. Fasting teaches self-control, discipline and patience. It also brings the people who fast closer to God. By sharing the hunger pain, they realize the need to share their fortune with the less fortunate. Fasting develops a keen sense of brotherhood among those who fast. Fasting also cleanses ones soul.

4. **Poor due or 'Zakat':** Every Muslim is obliged to pay annually 2½% of his cash savings and liquid assets like gold, silver, bonds etc. to his less fortunate fellow human beings (not necessarily to Muslims). This money is to be spent for the financial benefits of the needy, especially those who do not ask for help. Poor or needy close relatives get the first consideration. Thereafter the poor in the same neighborhood, then those in the society, the unemployed, the stranded traveler, and the new converts abandoned by their relatives. This is to be done very honorably, without any pride or any expectations of worldly gain from them. Willful sacrifice of one's personal wealth broadens one's heart and gets rid of miserly selfish attitudes. When call comes for greater sacrifice for God, Muslims come forward without hesitation.

5. **Pilgrimage or 'Hajj': Hajj is pilgrimage to Mecca in Saudi Arabia to worship at the Kaba (not to worship the Kaba itself!) and nearby Arafat to mark the occasion when Prophet Abraham (P) was willing to sacrifice his only son (Ishmael)** (Genesis 22:2). The Kaba is the "House of God" built by Abraham (P) in Mecca for the worship of one true God. The footprints of Abraham (P) are on the stone, which he used to build the Kaba, can be seen today next to the Kaba. The ZamZam well created by Ishmael is still there for the last 4000 years and millions of Muslims drink this water throughout the year. The hills of Safa and Marwa, where Hagar ran for help, is located next to the Kaba. It is obligatory for every pilgrim to run in the same way 7 times as Hagar did. The 3 places when Satan tried to whisper to Abraham (P) while he was going with his son Ishmael to sacrifice by God's order are still there where every pilgrim is required to throw stones. This is an obligation for a Muslim, once in a lifetime, if the person is financially and physically able to do so. It is a great spiritual journey. It demands intense devotion, control of passion, refrain from bloodshed and everything evil. **Every male, king or peasant, rich or poor, black or white, wears two pieces of white unstitched clothes**

to cover the body. Women wear their usual attire. They all stand side-by-side, shoulder-to-shoulder, and perform all the rituals. People from all walks of life and from all over the world get together in the true spirit of **Islamic brotherhood.** The journey leaves a very deep and lasting spiritual impression on the heart and soul of every person.

Misinterpretations by Media

Jihad is frequently discussed in the western media. **Jihad can mean any extra effort in the path of God; any personal struggle.** When one wants to lead a righteous and virtuous life, there is constant struggle against the evil desires within oneself. When one wants to raise a family in a less than desirable environment, he or she has to exert extra efforts constantly against the evil influence of the environment and the society. One often exerts extra efforts to please or obey God. All these are acts of Jihad. If an Islamic state is attacked from outside it is the duty of all Muslims to exert their utmost to defend themselves from the attack. This is also Jihad. Jihad is never to be waged to force anybody to choose a particular religion. On the contrary, it is to be waged in order to protect ones right to choose freely. Therefore, if there is a force in the world that tries to prevent a person from practicing this right, Jihad may lead to fighting the force that is trying to prevent him from exercising free will. Due to the constant and **deliberate misinterpretation in the western media,** the word 'Jihad' insights a panic reaction among the non-Muslims. **An unjust effort or war cannot be called Jihad.** Often times the news media of the western world reports **"Islamic terrorists".** These two words are mutually contradictory. One who is peaceful cannot be a terrorist, and one who is a terrorist cannot be peaceful. The same news media, when reporting on Northern Ireland, does not say **"Christian terrorists".** The Western media labels **"Fundamentalist"** to define extremism. If a person follows Islam, he should be a good example for the society to follow and benefit everybody. No one should put the blame on any religion if terrorism, injustice or evil acts occur. It is an **individual** who makes the choice; the entire **Religion** should not be blamed. Western media also creates the bias **that only "Arabs"** are connected to Muslims. Any person who speaks Arabic is called Arab. Only 18% of the world Muslim population is Arabs. The **remaining 82% of the Muslims** live in Asia, Africa, and Europe...everywhere in the world. A detailed study of Islam will show that **Islam is a complete and practical code of life for all humans.** In Islam all men are created equal. No one is superior to any other by virtue of race, color, social or economic status. God says in the Quran: **"Verily the most honored of you in the sight of God is (he who is) the most righteous of you"** (Quran 49:13).

Comparative Analysis: Judaism, Christianity and Islam on Woman

Status of Women

Christianity and Islam are the two largest religions in the world with over three billion (over 50%) of people. Compare the status of women in these two religions.

1a. **Bible:** "There is neither Jew nor Greek, there is neither slave nor free, there is neither male nor female; for you are all one in Christ Jesus (P) (Galatians 3:28).

1b. **Quran:** "And they (women) have rights similar to those (of men) over them in kindness, and men are a degree above them" (Quran 2:228). Such "a degree above" is maintenance and protection of woman by men, because of their physical and psychological makeup. It implies **no superiority or advantage before the law**. "Men are the protectors and maintainers of women because God has given the one more (strength) than the other" (Quran 4:34 & Ref. 39-pl7). Financial responsibility for the maintenance of his wife, and children, and needy relative especially women, rests on the men (Ref. 39-p23). This is actually one **advantage** that a Muslim woman has over a man.

2a. **Bible:** "…Neither was the man created for the woman; **but the woman for the man**" (1st Corinthians 11:8-9). **"Let your women keep silence in the churches:** for it is not permitted unto them to speak; but they are commanded to be under obedience, as also saith the law. And if they will learn anything, let them ask their husbands at home: for it is a shame for woman to speak in the church" (I Corinthians 14:34-35). "I permit no woman to teach or to have authority over men; **she is to keep silent"** (Timothy 2:12).

2b. **In Islam** women are encouraged to ask questions, even in the mosque. During the caliphate of Omar, a woman argued with him in the mosque, proved her point and caused him to declare in the presence of the people: "The woman is right and Omar is wrong." (Ref. 39-p24). Seeking knowledge is obligatory on every Muslim man and Muslim woman. (Mohammed).

3a. **Bible:** God said to woman after Eve gave the forbidden fruit to Adam: **"I will greatly multiply your pain in childbearing ... and he (husband) shall rule over you** (Genesis 3:16).

3b. In Islam the blame for eating from the forbidden tree is put to **both Adam and Eve.** God later **forgave both of them**. "Then learned Adam from his Lord words of inspiration, and Lord turned towards him; for He is Oft-returning, Most Merciful" (Quran 2:37).

4a. **Bible (the veil):** Any woman who prays and prophecies with her head unveiled dishonors her head - it is the same as if her head were **shaven**, for if a woman will not veil herself then she should cut off her hair. But if it is disgraceful for a woman to be shorn or shaven, let her wear a veil. (1 Corinthians 11:5). **Not glory of God:** For a man ought not to cover his head, since he is the image and glory of God, but woman is the glory of man, for man was not made for woman, but woman for man. (1 Corinthians 11:7).

4b. **Quran** does not order women's head to be shaved for not wearing head cover. It says: **"that they should draw their veils over their bosoms and not display their beauty "** (Quran 24:30-31). The veil in Islam is **not for glory of a man**, but for chastity and piousness; to obey God.

5a. **Bible:** "A bad wife brings humiliation, downcast looks, and a wounded heart. Slack of hand and weak of knee is the man whose wife fails to make him happy. Woman is the origin of sin, and it is through her that we all die. Do not leave a leaky cistern to drip or allow a bad wife to say what she likes. If she does not accept your control, divorce her and send her away" (Ecclesiastes 25:25).

5b. **Quran:** ". But consort with them in kindness, for if you hate them it may happen that you hate a thing wherein God has placed **much good**." (Quran 4:19).

6a. **Bible:** "I find more bitter than death the woman who is a snare, whose heart is a trap and whose hands are chains. The man who pleases God will escape her, but the sinner she will ensnare." "Look...Adding one thing to another to discover...I found one upright man among a thousand, but not one upright woman among them all." (Ecclesiastes 7:26-28).

6b. **Quran:** "And God sets forth... the wife of Pharaoh: behold she said: 'O my Lord! Build for me, in nearness to You, a mansion in the Garden, and save me from Pharaoh and his doings..."And Mary the daughter of Imran, who guarded her chastity... and she testified to the truth of the words of her Lord and of His Revelations, and was one of the devout." (Quran 66:11-2). "Heaven is at the feet of the mothers." (Mohammed).

7a. **Bible:** "If a father/husband does not endorse his daughter/wife's vows, all pledges made by her become null and void, in other words a woman cannot make any contract on her own without the permission of a husband or father: "but if her father forbids her when he hears about it, none of her vows or the pledges by which she obligated herself will stand.... Her husband may confirm or nullify any vow she makes or any sworn pledge to deny herself". (Numbers 30:2-15).

7b. **Quran**: "...and covet not the thing in which God has made some of you excel others. Unto men a fortune from that which they have earned, and unto women a fortune from that which they have earned..." (Quran 4:32).

8a. **Marriage: In Roman law,** women could not be a teacher, a surety, or a witness. She could not make any will or contracts. Anything a woman owned became the property of the husband after her marriage, including herself. **In the Mosaic Law,** the wife was betrothed: "To betroth a wife to oneself meant simply to acquire possession of her by payment of the purchase money; the betrothed is a girl for whom the purchase money has been paid" (Encyclopedia 1902, VOL. 3 - p 2942). The consent of the girl was <u>not</u> necessary for the validation of marriage: "The woman being man's property, his right to her follows as a matter of course." In the Mosaic Law it was a privilege of the husband only (Encyclopedia Biblica 11th Edition, p 782).

8b. In **Islam** women cannot be forced to marry anyone without their consent: "You are **forbidden to inherit women against their will"** (Quran 4:19). The Quran **orders husbands:** "Live with them on a footing of kindness and equity" (Quran 4:19).

9a. **Marriage by force: Bible:** "If brothers dwell together, and one of them dies and has no son, the wife of the dead shall not be married outside of the family to a stranger; her husband's brother shall go into her, and take her as his wife. (Deuteronomy 25:5)

9b. **Quran:** She can't be forced to marry. Even if parents, relatives, and everyone agree, and she does not, marriage can't happen: "You are forbidden to inherit women against their will" (Quran 4:19)

10a. **If he refuses? Bible:** "And if the man does not wish to take his brother's wife then his brother's wife shall go up to the gate of the elders, and say, "My husband's brother refuses to perpetuate his brother's name in Israel. Then the elders of his city shall call him. And if he persists, then his brother's wife shall go up to him in the presence of the elders, and pull his sandal off his foot, and spit in his face; and shall say: So it shall be done to the man who does not build up his brother's house. And the name of his house shall be called in Israel: 'The house of him that had his sandal pulled off.' (Deuteronomy 25:7).

10b. Quran: There is **no** forced marriage in Islam, in any case. (Quran 4:19)

11a. Bible: "After he left Hebron, David took more concubines and wives in Jerusalem, and more sons and daughters were born to him." (2 Samuel 5:13). He (Solomon) had 700 wives of royal birth and 300 concubines..." (1 Kings 11:3).

11b. Quran: "If you fear that you shall not be able to deal justly with the orphans, marry women of your choice, two, or three, or four; but if you fear that you shall not be able to deal justly (with them), **then only one...** to prevent you from doing injustice." (Quran 4:3). The Quran came down at a time when the culture allowed for multiple wives; it **limited** the number to four.

12a. Bible: "Do not take your wife's sister as a rival wife and have sexual relations with her while your wife is living." (Leviticus 18:18).

12b. Quran: "Prohibited to you (for marriage) are: - your mothers, daughters, sisters...and two sisters (the wife and her sister) in wedlock at one and the same time..." (Quran 4:23).

13a. Property Rights: English common law: "all real property which a wife held at the time of marriage became a possession of the husband" (Encyclopedia America Intl. Edition V29, p108). Married women's property act of England was passed in 1870 (Ref. 39-p8). France made woman eligible to contract in 1938, however the wife was still required to secure her husband's permission before she could dispose her private property (Ref. 39-p 21). Widows and sisters do not inherit at all. Daughters can inherit only if their deceased father had <u>no sons</u>. (Numbers 27:1-11).

13b. Islamic law Recognizes women's right to her money, real estate, or other properties. She has full rights to buy, sell, mortgage or lease any or all of her properties (Ref. 39-p 21). Women have the right to inheritance (Quran 4:7). Her share is hers and no one can make any claim on it (Ref. 39 - P22).

14a. Bible: "Say to the Israelites, 'If a man dies and leaves no son, turn his inheritance over to his daughter...'" (Numbers 27:8).

14b. Quran: "From what is left by parents and those nearest related there is a share for men **and** a share for women, whether the property be small or large, -a determinate share." (Quran 4:7).

15a. Status of Mother: Bible: "Children, obey your parents in everything, for this pleases the Lord." (Colossians 3:20). In the same Bible Jesus (P) addressed his mother a "woman": "And when they wanted wine, the mother of Jesus (P) saith unto him, 'They have no wine'. Jesus (P) saith unto her, **Woman, what have I to do with thee?** Mine hour is not yet come" (John 2:3-4).

15b. In Islam kindness to parents is considered next to worship of God: "your lord has decreed that you worship none save Him, and that you be **kind to your parents**" (Quran 17:23). Mohammad (P) said: **"Paradise is at the feet of the mother"** (Mohammad (P), Ref. 35-p 80). A man asked Muhammad (P): 'whom should I honor most?' The prophet replied: *'Your mother'*. 'And who comes next?' Asked the man. The prophet replied: *'Your mother'*. 'And who comes next?' Asked the man. The prophet replied: *'Your mother'*. 'And who comes next?' Asked the man. The prophet replied: *'Your father'* " (Mohammad (P)).

16a. Bible: "When a woman has her regular flow of blood, the impurity of her monthly period will last seven days, and anyone who touches her will be unclean till evening. Anything she lies on during her period will be unclean, and anything she sits on will be unclean. Whoever touches her bed must wash his clothes and bathe with water, and he will be unclean till evening. Whether it is the bed or anything she was sitting on, when anyone touches it, he will be unclean till evening." (Leviticus 15:19-23).

16b. Quran: Ali asked Mohammed if when a man and a woman make love and their clothes stick to them from the sweat of their bodies, or if a woman has her period and her clothes stick to her body, are the clothes considered unclean? Mohammad (P) replied: "No, the uncleanness is **only** in the semen and the blood itself."

17a. Bible: "Do not approach a woman to have sexual relations during the uncleanness of her monthly period." (Leviticus 18:19).

17b. Quran: "They ask you concerning women's period. Say: They are a hurt and a pollution: so keep away (making love) from women during their period, and do not approach them until they are clean..." (Quran 2:222).

18a. Postpartum: Bible: "...if a woman has **conceived** seed, and born a **man** child: then she shall be unclean **7 days**...but if she bear a **maid** child, then she shall be unclean **14 days**.."(Leviticus 12:2-5)

18b. Quran: "To God belongs the dominion of the heavens and the earth...He bestows female children to whomever He wills and bestows male children to whomever He wills. (Quran 42:49). "He who is involved in bringing up daughters, and accords benevolent treatment towards them, **they** (the daughters) will be **protection for him against Hell-Fire**." (Mohammed).

19a. Bible: "...the head of every man is Christ, and the head of the woman is man, and the head of Christ is God. Every man who prays or prophesies with his head covered dishonors his head...If a woman does not cover her head, she should have her hair cut off; and if it is a disgrace for a woman to have her hair cut or shaved off, she should cover her head" (1 Corinthians 11:3-6)". "I also want women to dress modestly, with decency and propriety, <u>not with braided hair</u> or gold or pearls or expensive clothes, but with good deeds, appropriate for women who profess to worship God"(1 Tim. 2:9-10)

19b. Quran: "O Prophet! Tell... the believing women, that they should cast their outer garments over their persons (when abroad): that is most convenient, that they should be known **and not molested...**" (Quran 33:59). ...They (believing women) should not display their beauty and ornaments except what (ordinarily) appear thereof; that they should draw their veils over their bosoms and not display their beauty **except to their husbands, their fathers, their husbands' fathers, their sons, their husbands' sons, their brothers or their brothers' sons, or their sisters' sons, or their women...or small children...**" (Quran 24:31).

20a. Bible: "..Anyone who divorces his wife and marries another woman commits adultery against her. And if she divorces her husband and marries another man, she commits adultery." (Mark 10:11-12).

20b. Quran: "O Prophet! When you do divorce women, divorce them at their prescribed periods, and count (accurately) their prescribed periods: and fear God your Lord..." (Quran 65:1). "If a wife fears cruelty or desertion on her husband's part, there is no blame on them if they arrange an **amicable** settlement between themselves; and such settlement is best" (Quran 4:128)

21a. Bible: "...who marries the divorced woman commits adultery." (Matthew 5:32). 'The woman he (the priest) marries must be a virgin. He must not marry a widow, a divorced woman, or a woman defiled by prostitution, but only a virgin from his own people.'" (Leviticus 21:13-4).

21b. Quran: "If any of you die and leave widows behind, they shall wait concerning themselves four months and ten days: when they have fulfilled their term, there is no blame on you (marrying widows) if they dispose of themselves in a just and reasonable manner..." (Quran 2:234). Most of the wives of Mohammad (P) were widowed, old, poor, and with nobody to take care of them. These women were good enough for the Prophet (P) to marry; they were **not** rejected.

22a. Bible: "Then he (Jesus (P)) went down to Nazareth with them (his parents) and was obedient to them..." (Luke 2:51). "For Moses (P) said, 'Honor your father and your mother,' and, 'anyone who curses his father or mother must be put to death." (Mark 7:10).

22b. Quran: "He (God) has made me (Jesus (P)) kind to my mother, and not overbearing or miserable." (Quran 19:32). "And We have enjoined on man (to be good) to his parents: in travail (pains of childbirth) upon travail his mother bore him, and in two years was his weaning: (hear the command), "Show gratitude to Me and to your parents: to Me is (your final) Goal." (Quran 31:14)

23a. After intercourse: Bible: If a man has an emission of semen, he shall bathe his whole body in water, and be unclean until the evening. Every garment and every skin on which the semen comes shall be washed with water, and be unclean until the evening. (Leviticus 15:16, 18)

23b: Quran: If he/she takes a bath where the whole body is cleaned with water, then he/she is clean: no need to wait till evening, no need to wash garments if not wet by semen. Intercourse is **not** viewed as an evil or dirty act in Islam; rather it is **encouraged between spouses** and incorporated into the religion itself.

Views of Canonized Saints in Christianity Concerning Women

1. "Woman is a daughter of falsehood, a sentinel of Hell, the enemy of peace; through her Adam lost paradise." (St. John Damascene Ref. 35-p79).

2. Woman is evil: "The leaden cover was lifted, there was a woman sitting, and he (the angel) said: this is wickedness." (Zech. 5:7)

3. "Woman is the instrument which the Devil uses to gain possession of our souls" (St. Cyprian Ref. 35-p79).

4. "Woman is the fountain of the arm of the Devil, her voice is the hissing of the serpent" (St. Anthony Ref. 35-p79).

5. "A virgin who is raped must marry her rapist (if they are *found*). "If a man happens to meet a virgin who is not pledged to be married and rapes her and they are discovered, he shall pay the girl's father fifty shekels of silver. He must marry the girl, for he has violated her. He can never divorce her as long as he lives" (Deuteronomy 22:28-30).

6. "Woman has the poison of an asp, the malice of a dragon". (St. Gregory the Great Ref. 35 - p79).

7. The Bible forbids divorce: "Every one who divorces his wife and marries another commits adultery, and he who marries a woman divorced from her husband commits adultery" (Luke 16:18).

8. Hebrew literature says: "No wickedness comes anywhere near the wickedness of a woman...Sin began with a woman and thanks to her we all must die" (Ecclesiastes 25:19,24).

9. Jewish Rabbis listed **nine** curses inflicted on women: "To the woman He gave nine curses and death: the burden of the blood of menstruation and the blood of virginity; the burden of pregnancy; the burden of childbirth; the burden of bringing up the children; her head is covered as one in mourning; she pierces her ear like a permanent slave or slave girl who serves her master; she is not to be believed as a witness; and after everything--death."

10. Orthodox Jewish men in their daily Morning Prayer recite, "Blessed be God King of the universe that Thou has not made me a woman." The women, on the other hand, thank God every morning for "making me according to Thy will."

11. Jewish prayer: "Praised be God that he has not created me a gentile. Praised be God that he has not created me a woman."

12. St. Paul in the New Testament: "A woman should learn in quietness and full submission. I do not permit a woman to teach or to have authority over a man; she must be silent. For Adam was formed first, then Eve. And Adam was not the one deceived; it was the woman who was deceived and became a sinner" (I Timothy 2:11-14).

13. St. Tertullian talking to 'best beloved sisters' in the faith, said: "Do you not know that you are each an Eve? The sentence of God on this sex of yours lives in this age: the guilt must of necessity live too. You are the Devil's gateway: You are the unsealer of the forbidden tree: You are the first deserter of the divine law: You are she who persuaded him whom the devil was not valiant enough to attack. You destroyed so easily God's image, man. On account of your desert even the Son of God had to die."

14. St. Augustine wrote to a friend: "What is the difference whether it is in a wife or a mother, it is still Eve the temptress that we must beware of in any woman.... I fail to see what use woman can be to man, if one excludes the function of bearing children."

15. St. Thomas Aquinas said: "As regards the individual nature, woman is defective and misbegotten, for the active force in the male seed tends to the production of a perfect likeness in the masculine sex; while the production of woman comes from a **defect** in the active

force or from some material indisposition, or even from some external influence."

16. 'Reformer' Martin Luther could not see any benefit from a woman: "If they become tired or even die, that does not matter. Let them die in childbirth, that's why they are there".

The Bible did **not** give the status that women in Christian countries reached today. It was achieved through long struggle and sacrifices on the part of women themselves and only when the society *needed* her contribution and work, especially during the two world wars (Ref. 39-P26). Even then, when one looks into the positions the women hold in business and political offices, the salary they receive, the sexual harassment they endure, the exploitation of women by the society for physical pleasure and promotion of business, 'equal rights' of women are not fully reached. She is bought (at a price), made to do things to satisfy the desires of the society and then sold to the adulterous "civilized" world, all in the name of progress, equal rights, women's liberation, economic freedom, commercial progress, and personal lifestyle.

Status and Responsibility of Women in Islam

Islam came at a time when women's rights was unheard of. The Pagan Arabs of the time indulged in practices such as buriying their daughters alive and marriying unlimited numbers of women (without taking responsibility). Islam was sent as a means of limitation for men regarding this issue and an emancipation for women. It raised women to respectful, righteous levels while giving them numerous rights (stated below). Still today, Muslim women enjoy these God-given rights. Compare a Muslim woman's rights with that of a Christian, Jewish, or Hindu woman's.

1. Women are exempted from obligatory daily prayers during their monthly periods and forty days after childbirth. Islam allows the woman to rest and care for her health first. They are also exempted during pregnancy and nursing a child if there is any threat to her health or to her baby.

2. Friday congregational prayer is mandatory for men but optional for woman.

3. Women have the full rights to her "Mahr", **a marriage gift,** and such ownership does **not** transfer to her husband or father. The marriage gift symbolizes man's respect, love and affection for the woman he is going to marry (Ref. 39-P17). The Quran says: "When you divorce a woman, do not take back anything that you have given her (however great it may be)" (Quran 4:20).

4. Islam emphasizes the importance of taking counsel and mutual agreement in family decisions: "If they (husband and wife) decide ... by mutual consent and (after) due consultation, there is no blame on them" (Quran 2:233).

5. **Protection of woman's honor:** The Quran says: "And those who launch a charge against chaste women, and not produce **four witnesses**, flog them with eighty stripes and reject their evidence ever after" (Quran 24:4). When a spouse is accused and no witness is presented, the witness of the woman to defend her honor and chastity is greater than the witness of the male accuser (Quran 24:6-9). Clearly Islam protects **(even legally)** women, even if there is a doubt about her innocence.

6. **Quran says:** "Say to the believing men that they should **lower their gaze and guard their modesty:** that will make for greater purity for them: ...And say to the believing women that they should lower their gaze and guard their modesty; that they should not display their beauty and ornaments except what (must ordinarily) appear thereof; that they should draw veils over their bosom and not display their beauty except to their husbands, their fathers ..." (Quran 24:30-31). Women in Islam are **respected for their minds**, not their bodies!

7. Islam declared women and men equal in most aspects and **complementary** in the remaining.

8. Islam condemned pre-Islamic practices degrading and oppressing women, such as burying daughters, etc.

9. The same injunctions and prohibitions of Islam equally apply to **both** sexes.

10. Islam gave women the right to accept or reject a marriage proposal free from pressure, and by mutual agreement to specify in the marriage contract that she has the **right to divorce**.

11. Islam does **not** require women to change their names at marriage; in fact, a woman should keep her father's last name in order to always maintain her identity. She is **not** the property of her husband!

12. Islam enjoins sound morality in thinking, behavior and appearance. Dress fashions and social patterns that reduce woman to a sex object and exploit her as such are **not acceptable** to Islam.

13. Islam protects the family and condemns the betrayal of marital fidelity. It recognizes only one type of family: husband and wife united by authentic marriage contract.

14. Both men and women have **equal right** to seek an end to an **unsuccessful marriage.** To protect from hasty decision out of temporary emotional stress, certain steps and waiting periods are observed (Ref. 39-P19). She bears no obligation to spend from her property on her husband or family, even if she works. She bears no financial responsibility to maintain her children.

15. If divorced, she may also get alimony from her ex-husband.

16. Islam gave women right of inheritance and the right of individual independent ownership unhampered by the father, husband, brother, son, or anyone else.

17. There is no law in Islam that forbids women to seek employment. In fact, a woman named Khadija employed Mohammad (P).

18. **Advise of Mohammad (P):** "You have certain rights over your women, but **they also have rights over you**...do treat your women well and be kind to them for they are your partners and committed helpers" (Mohammad (P)'s last sermon).

    • **"Best of you are those who are kindest with your wives"** (Ref. 39-pl8).

    • **"It is the generous who are good to women,** and it is the wicked who insults them" (Ref. 39-p2l).

    • "Heaven is at the feet of mothers" (Mohammad (P)).

    • Islam equally demands the observance of chastity and moral standards from **both men and women.** "Women are the siblings of men" (Mohammad (P)).

19. "For Muslim...believing men **and women,** for devout men **and women,** for true men **and women,** for men **and women** who are patient, for men **and women** who humble themselves, for men **and women** who give in charity, for men **and women** who fast, for men **and women** who guard their chastity, and for men **and women** who engage much in God's praise- For **them all** has God prepared **forgiveness and great reward"** (Quran 33:35).

20. "The believers, **men and women,** are protectors, one of another: they enjoin what is just, and forbid what is evil, they observe regular prayers, practice regular charity, and obey God and His Messenger. On them will God pour His Mercy: for God is Exalted in power, Wise" (Quran 9:71).

21. "And their Lord answered them: Truly I will never cause to be lost the work of any of you, **Be you a male or female,** you are members one of another" (Quran 3:195).

22. "...whoever works a righteous deed -**whether man or woman**- and is a believer- such will enter the Garden of bliss". (Quran 40:40)

23. "Whoever works righteousness, **man or woman**, and has faith, verily to him/her we will give a new life that is good and pure, and we will bestow on such their reward according to the best of their actions" (Quran 16:97).

The Quranic view of women is no different than that of men. Both are God's creatures whose sublime goal on earth is to worship their Lord, do righteous deeds, and avoid evil and they, *both*, will be assessed accordingly. The Quran **never** mentions that the woman is the devil's gateway or that she is a deceiver by nature. Also, The Quran never mentions that man is God's image; it states that all men and all women are his creatures, simple as that. According to the Quran, a woman's role on earth is not limited only to childbirth. She is required to do as many good deeds as any other man is required to do. The Quran **never** says that no upright women have ever existed. On the contrary, God has created some women so pious that the Quran has instructed **all the believers**, women **as well as men**, to follow the example of those ideal women such as the Virgin Mary and Pharoah's wife.

Mothers

1. Old Testament commands kind and considerate treatment towards parents and condemns those who dishonor them. For example, "If anyone curses his father or mother, he must be put to death" (Leviticus 20:9) and "A wise man brings joy to his father but a foolish man despises his father" (Proverbs 15:20). Honoring the father alone is mentioned in some places: "A wise man heeds his father's instruction" (Proverbs 13:1), the mother without mention of father is never mentioned. There is no special emphasis on treating the mother kindly as a sign of appreciation of her great suffering in childbearing and suckling. Also, mothers do not inherit at all from their children while fathers do.

2. The New Testament considers kind treatment of mothers as an impediment to the way to God. According to the New Testament, one cannot become a good Christian worthy of becoming a disciple of Christ unless he hates his mother. It is attributed to Jesus (P) to have said: "If anyone comes to me and does not hate his father and mother, his wife and children, his brothers and sisters--yes, even his own life-- he can not be my disciple" (Luke 14:26).

3. The New Testament depicts a picture of Jesus (P) as indifferent to, or even disrespectful of, his own mother. For example, when she had come looking for him while he was preaching to a crowd, he did n care to go out to see her: "Then Jesus (P)' mother and brothers arrive Standing outside, they sent someone to call him. A crowd was sittin around him and they told him, 'Your mother and brothers are outsic looking for you.' 'Who are my mother and my brothers?' he aske Then he looked at those seated in a circle around him and said: 'He are my mother and my brothers! Whoever does God's will is n brother and sister and mother.' (Mark 3:31-35).

4. One might argue that Jesus (P) was trying to teach his audience a important lesson that religious ties are no less important than fami ties. However, he could have taught his listeners the same lessc without showing such absolute indifference to his mother. The san disrespectful attitude is depicted when he refused to endorse statement made by a member of his audience blessing his mother role in giving birth to him and nursing him: "As Jesus (P) was sayir these things, a woman in the crowd called out, 'Blessed is the moth who gave you birth and nursed you.' He replied, 'Blessed rather a those who hear the word of God and obey it." (Luke 11:27-28). If son of the stature of Jesus Christ had treated a mother with the statu of the Virgin Mary with such discourtesy, as depicted in the Ne Testament, then how should average Christian sons treat averag Christian mothers?

5. In Islam, the honor, respect, and esteem attached to motherhood a unparalleled. The Quran places the importance of kindness to paren as second only to worshipping God Almighty: "Your Lord h decreed that you worship none but Him, and that you be kind parents. Whether one or both of them attain old age in your life, S not to them a word of contempt, nor repel them, but address them terms of honor. And out of kindness, lower to them the wing humility, and say: 'My Lord! Bestow on them Your Mercy as th cherished me in childhood' " (Quran 17:23-24).

6. The Quran emphasizes a mother's great role in giving birth ar nursing: "And We have enjoined on man to be good to his parents: travail upon travail did his mother bear him and in two years was h weaning. Show gratitude to Me and to your parents" (Quran 31:14).

7. "A man asked Mohammad (P): 'Whom should I honor most?' T Prophet replied: 'Your mother'. 'And who comes next?' asked the ma The Prophet replied: 'Your mother'. 'And who comes next?' asked t man. The Prophet replied: 'Your mother!' 'And who comes nex asked the man. The Prophet replied: 'Your father'" (Mohammad (P)).

Shameful Daughters?

1. The Bible states explicitly: "The birth of a daughter is a loss" (Eccles. 22:3). In contrast, boys receive special praise: "A man who educates his son will be the envy of his enemy." (Ecclesiastics 30:3).

2. Jewish Rabbis made preference to male children: "It is well for those whose children are male but ill for those whose are female", "At the birth of a boy, all are joyful...at the birth of a girl all are sorrowful", and "When a boy comes into the world, peace comes into the world... When a girl comes, nothing comes."

3. A daughter is considered a painful burden, a shame on her father: "Your daughter is headstrong? Keep a sharp look-out that she does not make you the laughing stock of your enemies, the talk of the town, the object of common gossip, and put you to public shame" (Ecclesiastics 42:11).

4. "Keep a headstrong daughter under firm control, or she will abuse any indulgence she receives. Keep a strict watch on her shameless eye, do not be surprised if she disgraces you" (Ecclesiastics 26:10-11).

5. It was this very same idea of treating daughters as sources of shame that led the pagan Arabs, **before the advent of Islam**, to practice female infanticide. This sinister crime would have never stopped in Arabia were it not for the power of the scathing terms the Quran used to condemn this practice (Quran 16:59, 43:17, 81:8-9). The Quran makes no distinction between boys and girls. The Quran even mentions the gift of the female birth first: "...He bestows female children to whomever He wills and bestows male children to whomever He wills" (Quran 42:49). In order to wipe out all the traces of female infanticide in the society, Muhammad (P) promised: "Whoever maintains two girls till they attain maturity, he and I will come on the Resurrection Day like this; and he joined his fingers". (Mohammed).

Female Education?

1. According to the Talmud, "women are exempt from the study of the Torah." Some Jewish Rabbis firmly declared, "Let the words of Torah rather be destroyed by fire than imparted to women", and "Whoever teaches his daughter Torah, it is as though he taught her obscenity".

2. St. Paul: "...women should remain silent in the churches." (I Corinthians 14:34-35). How can a woman learn if she is not allowed to speak or ask questions? How can she broaden her horizons if her one and only source of information is her **husband** at home?

3. One short story narrated in the Quran sums up its position on education: Khawlah was a Muslim woman whose husband Aws pronounced with anger: "You are to me as the back of my mother." This was held by pagan Arabs to be a statement of divorce that freed the husband from any conjugal responsibility but did not leave the wife free to leave the husband's home or to marry another man. She went straight to Mohammed (P) to plead her case. The Prophet asked her to be patient. Khawla kept pleading with the Prophet to save her suspended marriage. Shortly, the Quran intervened: Khawla's plea was accepted. The divine verdict abolished this iniquitous custom. One full chapter (# 58) of the Quran whose title is "Almujadilah" or "The woman who is arguing" was named after this incident: "God has **heard and accepted** the statement of the woman who pleads with you (the Prophet) concerning her husband and…God hears and sees all things...." (Quran 58:1). A woman has the right to argue even with the Prophet of Islam himself. No one has the right to instruct her to be silent. She is under no obligation to consider her husband to be the one and only reference in matters of law and religion, in fact, if he orders something against Islam, she should disregard his words.

Unclean, Impure Women?

1. The Old Testament considers any menstruating woman as unclean and impure. Her impurity "infects" others as well: "When a woman has her regular flow of blood, the impurity of her monthly period will last seven days, and anyone who touches her will be unclean till evening. Anything she lies on during her period will be unclean, and anything she sits on will be unclean. Whoever touches her bed must wash his clothes and bathe with water, and he will be unclean till evening. Whoever touches anything she sits on must wash his clothes and bathe with water, and he will be unclean till evening. Whether it is the bed or anything she was sitting on, when anyone touches it, he will be unclean till evening" (Leviticus 15:19-23).

2. Due to her "contaminating" nature, she is "banished" in order to avoid any possibility of contact with her. She was sent to a special house called "house of uncleanness" for the whole period of her 'impurity'. The Talmud considers a menstruating woman "fatal" even without any physical contact: "… if a menstruate woman passes between two (men), if it is at the beginning of her menses she will slay one of them, and if it is at the end of her menses she will cause strife between them" (bPes. 111a.).

3. The <u>husband</u> of a menstruating woman was forbidden to enter the synagogue if he was made unclean by her even by the dust under her feet. A priest whose wife, daughter, or mother was menstruating could not recite priestly blessing in the synagogue.

4. Islam does not consider a menstruating woman to possess any kind of "contagious uncleanness". She is neither "untouchable" nor "cursed." She practices her normal life with only one restriction: A married couple is not allowed to have sexual intercourse during the period of menstruation. Any physical contact between them is **permissible**. A menstruating woman is exempted from daily prayers and fasting during her period. This is due to hormonal changes, discomfort, etc.

Bearing Witness

1. Quran has instructed the believers dealing in financial transactions to get two male witnesses or one male and two females (2:282). The reasoning for this is that since women were primarily in the house and had limited interaction or dealings with these issues, common sense dictates that she will probably have less knowledge than a man on this issue. Also, in situations where a woman's testimony is half of the man's, God has **decreed this to protect the woman**, because it was extremely dangerous to be a witness in that time. (No 'witness protection' programs). To protect the woman, it was safer if she testified alongside another witness. This rule in **no way** implies that a woman is less intelligent than a man. The Quran in other situations accepts the testimony of a woman as equal to that of a man. In fact the woman's testimony can even **invalidate the man's**. If a man accuses his wife of unchastity, he is required by the Quran to solemnly swear five times as evidence of the wife's guilt. If the wife denies and swears similarly five times, she is **not considered guilty** and in either case the marriage is dissolved. (Quran 24:6-11).

2. In early Jewish society, women were not allowed to bear witness. The Rabbis counted women's not being able to bear witness among the nine curses inflicted upon all women because of the Fall. Women in today's Israel are not allowed to give evidence in Rabbinical courts. The Rabbis justify why women cannot bear witness by citing Genesis 18:9-16, where it says that Sara, Abraham (P)'s wife, had lied. The Rabbis use this incident as evidence that women are unqualified to bear witness. It should be noted here that this story narrated in Genesis 18:9-16 has been mentioned more than once in the Quran **without any hint** of any lies by Sara (Quran 11:69-74, 51:24-30). In

the Christian West, both ecclesiastical and civil law debarred women from giving testimony until late last century!

3. If a man accuses his wife of unchastity, her testimony will not be considered at all according to the Bible. The accused wife has to be subjected to a trial by ordeal. In this trial, the wife faces a complex and humiliating ritual, which is supposed to prove her guilt or innocence (Num. 5:11-31). If she is found guilty after this ordeal, she will be sentenced to death. If she is found not guilty, her husband will be innocent of any wrongdoing.

4. "If a man takes a wife and, after lying with her... saying, 'I married this woman, but when I approached her, I did not find proof of her virginity,' then the girl's father and mother shall bring proof that she was a virgin to the town elders at the gate. The girl's father...'shall display the cloth before the elders of the town, and the elders shall take the man and punish him. They shall fine him a hundred shekels of silver and give them to the girl's father, because this man has given an Israelite virgin a bad name. She shall continue to be his wife; he must not divorce her as long as he lives. If, however, the charge is true and no proof of the girl's virginity can be found, she shall be brought to the door of her father's house and there the men of the town shall **stone her to death**. She has done a disgraceful thing in Israel by being promiscuous while still in her father's house. You must purge the evil from among you." (Deuteronomy 22:13-21)

Adultery

1. Adultery is considered a sin in all religions. The Bible decrees the death sentence for both the adulterer and the adulteress (Leviticus 20:10). Islam equally punishes **both** the adulterer and the adulteress (Quran 24:2). The Quranic definition of adultery is very different from the Biblical definition. According to Quran, Adultery is the involvement of a married man or a married woman in an extramarital affair. The Bible only considers extramarital affair of a married woman as adultery (Leviticus 20:10, Deut. 22:22, Proverbs 6:20-7:27)

2. "If a man is found sleeping with another man's wife, both the man who slept with her and the woman must die. You must purge the evil from Israel" (Deuteronomy 22:22, Leviticus 20:10).

3. According to the Biblical definition, if a married man sleeps with an unmarried woman, this is **not considered a crime at all.** The married man who has extramarital affairs with unmarried women is not an adulterer and the unmarried women involved with him are not adulteresses. The crime of adultery is committed only when a man,

whether married or single, sleeps with a married woman! In this case the man is considered adulterer, and the woman is considered adulteress. Why is there a double dual moral standard? According to Encyclopedia Judaic, the wife was considered to be the husband's possession and adultery constituted a violation of the husband's exclusive right to her; the wife as the husband's possession had no such right to him. So if a man had sexual intercourse with a married woman, he would be violating the property of another man and, thus, he should be punished.

4. To this present day in Israel, if a married man indulges in an extramarital affair with an unmarried woman, his children by that woman are considered legitimate. But, if a married woman has an affair with another man, whether married or not married, her children by that man are not only illegitimate but they are considered bastards and are forbidden to marry any other Jews except converts and other bastards. This ban is **handed down to the children's descendants for 10 generations** until taint of adultery is presumably weakened.

5. The Quran, on the other hand, never considers any woman to be the possession of any man. The Quran eloquently describes the relationship between the spouses by saying: "And among His signs is that He created for you mates from among yourselves, that you may dwell in tranquility with them and He has put love and mercy between your hearts: verily in that are signs for those who reflect" (Quran 30:21). This is the Quranic conception of marriage: love, mercy, and tranquility, not possession and double standards.

Vows

1. According to the Bible, a man must fulfill any vows he might make to God. On the other hand, a woman's vow is not necessarily binding on her. It has to be approved **by her father**, if she is living in his house, or **by her husband**, if she is married. If a father/husband does not endorse his daughter/wife's vows, all pledges made by her become null and void: "But if her father forbids her when he hears about it, none of her vows or the pledges by which she obligated herself will stand.... Her husband may confirm or nullify any vow she makes or any sworn pledge to deny herself" (Num. 30:2-15).

2. Why is it that a woman's word is not binding? The answer is simple: because her father owns her, before marriage, or her husband owns her after marriage. The father's control over his daughter was absolute to the extent that, should he wish, he could sell her! It is indicated in the writings of the Rabbis that: "The man may sell his daughter, but

the woman may not sell her daughter; the man may betroth his daughter, but the woman may not betroth her daughter." The Rabbinical literature also indicates that marriage represents transfer of control from the father to the husband: "betrothal, making a woman the sacrosanct possession... inviolable property...of the husband..." So, if the woman is considered to be the property of someone else, she cannot make any pledges that her owner does not approve!

3. This Biblical instruction concerning women's vows had negative repercussions on Judeo-Christian women till early in this century. A married woman had no legal status. Her husband could repudiate any contract, bargain, or deal she had made. Women were held unable to make a binding contract because they were practically owned by someone else. Western women had suffered for almost 2,000 years.

4. In Islam, the vow of every Muslim, male or female, is binding on him/her. No one has the power to repudiate the pledges of anyone else. Failure to keep a solemn oath, made by a man or a woman, has to be expiated as indicated in the Quran: "He (God) will call you to account for your deliberate oaths: for expiation, feed ten indigent persons, on a scale of the average for the food of your families; Or clothe them; or give a slave his freedom. If that is beyond your means, fast for three days. That is the expiation for the oaths you have sworn. But keep your oaths". (Quran 5:89).

5. Companions of Muhammad (P), men and women, used to present their oath of allegiance to him personally: "O Prophet, When believing women come to you to make a covenant with you that they will not associate in worship anything with God, nor steal, nor fornicate, nor kill their own children, nor slander anyone, nor disobey you in any just matter, then make a covenant with them and pray to God for the forgiveness of their sins. Indeed God is Forgiving and most Merciful" (Quran 60:12). A man could not swear the oath on behalf of his daughter or his wife. Nor could a man repudiate the oath made by any of his female relatives.

Wife's Property

1. The Jewish tradition regarding the husband's role towards his wife stems from the conception that he owns her as he owns his slave. This conception has been the reason behind the double standard in the laws of adultery and behind the husband's ability to annul his wife's vows. This conception has also been responsible for denying the wife any control over her property or her earnings. As soon as a Jewish woman got married, she completely loses any control over her property and

earnings to her husband. Thus, marriage caused the richest woman to become practically penniless. The Talmud describes the financial situation of a wife as follows: "How can a woman have anything; whatever is hers belongs to her husband? What is his is his and what is hers is also his... Her earnings and what she may find in the streets are also his. The household articles, even the crumbs of bread on the table, are his. Should she invite a guest to her house and feed him, she would be stealing from her husband..." (San. 71a, Git. 62a).

2. The fact of the matter is that the property of a Jewish female was meant to attract suitors. A Jewish family would assign their daughter a share of her father's estate to be used as a dowry in case of marriage. It was this dowry that made Jewish daughters an unwelcome burden to their fathers. The father had to raise his daughter for years and then prepare for her marriage by providing a large dowry. Thus, a girl in a Jewish family was a liability and not an asset. This liability explains why the birth of a daughter was not celebrated with joy in the old Jewish society. The dowry was wedding gift presented to the groom under terms of tenancy. The husband would act as the practical owner of the dowry but he could not sell it. The bride would lose any control over the dowry at the moment of marriage. She was expected to work after marriage and all her earnings had to go to her husband in return for her maintenance, which was his obligation. She could regain her property only in two cases: divorce or her husband's death. Should she die first, he would inherit her property. In case of the husband's death, the wife could regain her pre-marital property but she was not entitled to inherit any share in her deceased husband's own property.

3. Christianity, until recently, has followed the same Jewish tradition. Both religious and civil authorities in the Christian Roman Empire (after Constantine) required a property agreement as a condition for recognizing the marriage. Families offered their daughters increasing dowries and, as a result, men tended to marry earlier while families postponed their daughters' marriages until later than had been customary. Under Canon law, a wife was entitled to restitution of her dowry if the marriage was annulled unless she was guilty of adultery. In this case, she forfeited her right to the dowry, which remained in her husband's hands. Under Canon and civil law a married woman in Christian Europe and America had lost her property rights until late 19th and early 20th centuries. Moreover, she could not sue or be sued in her own name, nor could she sue her own husband. A married woman was practically treated as an infant in the eyes of the law. The wife simply belonged to her husband and therefore she lost her property, her legal personality, and her family name.

4. **Islam**, from 7th century, has granted married women an independent personality, which the Judeo-Christian tradition had deprived them until very recently. In Islam, the bride and her family are under no obligation whatsoever to present a gift to the groom. The girl in a Muslim family is no liability. A woman is so dignified by Islam that she does not need to present gifts in order to attract potential husbands. It is the groom who must present the bride with a marriage gift. This gift is considered her property and neither the groom nor the bride's family have any share or control over it. The bride retains her marriage gifts even if she is later divorced. The husband is not allowed any share in his wife's property except what she offers him with her free consent. The Quran has stated clearly: "And give the women (on marriage) their dower as a free gift; but if they, Of their own good pleasure, remit any part of it to you, take it and enjoy it with right good cheer" (Quran 4:4).

5. The wife's property and earnings are under her full control and for her use alone since her, and the children's, maintenance is her husband's responsibility. No matter how rich the wife might be, she is not obliged to act as a co-provider for the family unless she herself voluntarily chooses to do so. Moreover, a married woman in Islam retains her independent legal personality and her family name. An American judge once commented on the rights of Muslim women saying: "**A Muslim girl may marry ten times, but her individuality is not absorbed by that of her various husbands. She is a solar planet with a name and legal personality of her own**."

Divorce

1. Christianity abhors divorce altogether. The New Testament unequivocally advocates the indissolubility of marriage. It is attributed to Jesus (P) to have said: "But I tell you that anyone who divorces his wife, except for marital unfaithfulness, causes her to become adulteress, and anyone who marries the divorced woman commits adultery" (Matthew 5:32). This uncompromising ideal is, without a doubt, unrealistic. It assumes a state of moral perfection that human societies have never achieved. When a couple realizes that their married life is beyond repair, a ban on divorce will not do them any good. Forcing ill-mated couples to remain together against their wills is neither effective nor reasonable.

2. Judaism, at the other extreme, allows divorce even without any cause. The Old Testament gives the husband the right to divorce his wife even if he just dislikes her: "If a man marries a woman who

becomes displeasing to him because he finds something indecent about her, and he writes her a certificate of divorce, gives it to her and sends her from his house, and if after she leaves his house she becomes the wife of another man, and her second husband dislikes her and writes her a certificate of divorce, gives it to her and sends her from his house, or if he dies, then her first husband, who divorced her, is not allowed to marry her again after she has been defiled". (Deut. 24:1-4)

3. The above verses have caused debate among Jewish scholars because of their disagreement over the interpretation of the words "displeasing", "indecency", and "dislikes" mentioned. The Talmud records different opinions: "The school of Shammai held that a man should not divorce his wife unless he has found her guilty of some sexual misconduct, while the school of Hillel say he may divorce her even if she has merely spoiled a dish for him. Rabbi Akiba says he may divorce her even if he simply finds another woman more beautiful than she". (Gittin 90a-b).

4. The New Testament follows the Shammaites opinion while Jewish law has followed the opinion of the Hillelites and R. Akiba. Since the Hillelites' view prevailed, it became the unbroken tradition of Jewish law. The Old Testament not only gives the husband the right to divorce his "displeasing" wife, it considers divorcing a "bad wife" an obligation: "A bad wife brings humiliation, downcast looks, and a wounded heart. Slack of hand and weak of knee is the man whose wife fails to make him happy. Woman is the origin of sin, and it is through her that we all die. Do not leave a leaky cistern to drip or allow a bad wife to say what she likes. If she does not accept your control, divorce her and send her away". (Ecclesiastics 25:25).

5. The Talmud has recorded several specific actions by wives which obliged their husbands to divorce them: "If she ate in the street, if she drank greedily in the street, if she suckled in the street, in every case Rabbi Meir says that she must leave her husband" (Git. 89a). The Talmud also says: "... If a man took a wife and lived with her for ten years and she bore no child, he shall divorce her" (Yeb. 64a).

6. Under Jewish law, wives cannot initiate divorce. However, a wife could claim the right to a divorce before a Jewish court provided that a strong reason exists. Very few grounds are allowed: a husband with physical defects or skin disease, a husband not fulfilling his conjugal responsibilities, etc. The Court might support the wife's claim to a divorce but it cannot dissolve the marriage. The Court could scourge, fine, imprison, and excommunicate him to force him to deliver the

necessary bill of divorce to his wife. Only the husband can dissolve the marriage by giving his wife a bill of divorce. However, if the husband is stubborn enough, he can refuse to grant his wife a divorce and keep her tied to him indefinitely. Worse still, he can desert her without granting her a divorce and leave her both unmarried *and* undivorced. He can marry another woman or even live with any single woman out of wedlock and have children from her (these children are legitimate under Jewish law). The deserted wife, on the other hand, cannot marry any other man since she is still legally married and she cannot live with any other man because she will be considered an adulteress and her children from this union will be illegitimate for ten generations. A woman in such a position is called an **agunah** (chained woman). In the USA today there are about 1000 to 1500 Jewish women who are **agunot** (plural for agunah), while in Israel their number might be as high as 16000. Husbands may extort thousands of dollars from their trapped wives in exchange for a Jewish divorce.

7. **Islam** occupies the middle ground between Christianity and Judaism with respect to divorce. Marriage in Islam is a sanctified bond that should not be broken except for compelling reasons. Couples are instructed to pursue all possible remedies whenever their marriages are in danger. Divorce is not to be resorted to except when there is no other way out. In a nutshell, Islam recognizes divorce, yet it highly discourages it by all means. Islam does recognize the right of both partners to end their matrimonial relationship. Islam gives husband the right for divorce. Moreover, Islam, unlike Judaism, grants the wife the right to dissolve the marriage through what is known as Khula. If the husband dissolves the marriage by divorcing his wife, he cannot retrieve any of the marriage gifts he has given her.

8. In the case of the wife choosing to end the marriage, she may return the marriage gifts to her husband. Returning the marriage gifts in this case is a fair compensation for the husband who is keen to keep his wife while she chooses to leave him. The Quran says: "It is not lawful for you (Men) to take back any of your gifts except when both parties fear that they would be unable to keep the limits ordained by God. There is no blame on either of them if she gives something for her freedom. These are the limits ordained by God so do not transgress them" (Quran 2:229).

9. A woman came to Muhammad (P) seeking the dissolution of her marriage; she told the Prophet (P) that she did not have any complaints against her husband's character or manners. Her only problem was that she honestly did not like him to the extent of not

being able to live with him any longer. The Prophet (P) asked her: "Would you give him his garden (the marriage gift he had given her) back?" she said: "Yes". The Prophet then instructed the man to take back his garden and accept the dissolution of the marriage.

10. In some cases, A Muslim wife might be willing to keep her marriage but find herself obliged to claim for a divorce because of some compelling reasons such as: Cruelty of husband, desertion without a reason, a husband not fulfilling his conjugal responsibilities, etc. In these cases the Muslim court makes it easy to dissolve the marriage.

11. Islam has offered the Muslim woman some unequalled rights: she can end the marriage through Khula' and she can sue for a divorce. A recalcitrant husband can never chain a Muslim wife. It was these rights that enticed Jewish women who lived in the early Islamic societies of the 7th century to seek to obtain bills of divorce from their Jewish husbands in **Muslim courts**. The Rabbis declared these bills null and void. In order to end this practice, the Rabbis gave new rights and privileges to Jewish women in an attempt to weaken the appeal of the Muslim courts. Jewish women living in Christian countries were not offered any similar privileges since the Roman divorce law practiced there was no more attractive than Jewish law.

12. Islam discourages divorce. Mohammad (P) said: "Among all the permitted acts, divorce is the most hateful to God". Quran instructs: "Live with them (wives) on a footing of kindness and equity. If you dislike them it may be that you dislike something in which God has placed a great deal of good" (Quran 4:19). Prophet Muhammad (P) said: "A believing man must not hate a believing woman. If he dislikes one of her traits he will be pleased with another". The Prophet (P) has also emphasized: "The believers who show the most perfect faith are those who have the best character and the best of you are those who are best to their wives".

13. However, **Islam is a practical religion** and it *does* recognize that there are circumstances in which a marriage is about to collapse. In such cases, a mere advice of kindness or self-restraint is no viable solution. The Quran offers some practical advice for the spouse (husband or wife) whose partner (wife or husband) is the wrongdoer. For the husband whose wife's ill-conduct is threatening the marriage, the Quran gives four types of advice: "As to those women on whose part you fear disloyalty and ill-conduct, (1) Admonish them, (2) refuse to share their beds, (3) beat them; but if they return to obedience seek not against them means of annoyance: For God is Most High, Great. (4) If you fear a break between them, appoint two

arbiters, one from his family and the other from hers; If they wish for peace, God will cause their reconciliation" (Quran 4:34-35). The first three are to be tried first. If they fail, then the help of the families concerned should be sought. It should be noted that "beating" (a slight tap with a miswak—used to brush teeth with) the rebellious wife is a temporary measure that is resorted to as **third** in line in cases of extreme necessity in hopes that it might remedy the wrongdoing of the wife. If it does, the husband is not allowed by any means to continue any annoyance to the wife as explicitly mentioned in the verse. If it does not, the husband is still not allowed to use this measure any longer and the final avenue of the family-assisted reconciliation has to be explored.

14. Muhammad (P) has instructed Muslim husbands that they should not have recourse to these measures except in extreme cases: "In case they are guilty of open lewdness you may leave them alone in their beds and inflict **slight** punishment. If they are obedient to you, do not seek against them any means of annoyance". The Prophet of Islam has condemned any unjustifiable beating. Some Muslim wives complained to him that their husbands had beaten them. Hearing this, the Prophet (P) categorically stated that: "Those who do so (beat their wives) are **not** the best among you".

15. Talmud sanctions wife beating as chastisement for the purpose of discipline. The husband is not restricted to the extreme cases such as those of open lewdness. He is allowed to beat his wife *even if she just refuses to do her housework*. Moreover, he is not limited only to the use of 'light punishment'. He is permitted to break his wife's stubbornness by the lash or by starving her.

16. For the wife whose husband's ill-conduct is the cause for the marriage's near collapse, the Quran offers this advice: "If a wife fears cruelty or desertion on her husband's part, there is no blame on them if they arrange an **amicable** settlement between themselves; and such settlement is best" (Quran 4:128).

17. It should be noted that the Quran is not advising the **wife** to resort to the two measures of abstention from sex and beating. The reason for this disparity might be to protect the wife from a violent physical reaction by her already misbehaving husband. Such a violent physical reaction will do both the wife and the marriage more harm than good. The court can apply these measures against the husband on the wife's behalf: first admonishes the rebellious husband, then forbids him his wife's bed, and finally executes a symbolic beating.

18. Islam offers Muslim married couples much viable advice to save their marriages in cases of trouble and tension. If one of the partners is jeopardizing the matrimonial relationship, the other partner is advised by the Quran to do whatever possible and effective in order to save this sacred bond. If all the measures fail, Islam allows the partners to separate peacefully and amicably.

Female Inheritance

1. The Biblical attitude towards female inheritance has been succinctly described by Rabbi Epstein: "The continuous and unbroken tradition since the Biblical days gives the female members of the household, wife and daughters, **no right of succession** to the family estate. In the more primitive scheme of succession, the female members of the family were considered **part of the estate** and as remote from the legal personality of an heir as the slave. "They are owned --before marriage, by the father; after marriage, by the husband."

2. The Biblical rules of inheritance are outlined in Numbers 27:1-11. A wife is given no share in her husband's estate, while he is her first heir, even before her sons. A daughter can inherit only if no male heirs exist. A mother is not an heir at all while the father is. Widows and daughters, in case male children remained, were at the mercy of the male heirs for provision. That is why widows and orphan girls were among the most destitute members of the Jewish society.

3. Christianity has followed suit for a long time. Both the ecclesiastical and civil laws of Christendom barred daughters from sharing with their brothers in father's patrimony. Wives were deprived of any inheritance rights. These iniquitous laws survived till late 19th century.

4. Among the pagan Arabs **before Islam**, inheritance rights were confined exclusively to the male relatives. The Quran abolished all these unjust customs and gave all the female relatives inheritance shares: "From what is left by parents and those nearest related there is a share for men and a share for women, whether the property be small or large --a determinate share" (Quran 4:7).

5. Muslim mothers, wives, daughters, and sisters had received inheritance rights **1,300 years before the West** recognized that these rights even existed. The division of inheritance is a vast subject with an enormous amount of details (Quran 4:7,11,12,176). The general rule is that the female share is half the male's except the cases in which the mother receives equal share to that of the father. This general rule if taken in isolation from other legislations concerning men and women may seem unfair. In order to understand the rationale

behind this rule, one must take into account the fact that the financial obligations of men in Islam **far exceed** those of women. A bridegroom must provide his bride with a marriage gift. This gift becomes her exclusive property and remains so even if she is later divorced. The bride is under no obligation to present any gifts to her groom. Moreover, the Muslim husband is charged with the maintenance of his wife and children. The wife, on the other hand, is not obliged to help him in this regard. Her property and earnings are for her use alone except what she may voluntarily offer her husband. Besides, one has to realize that Islam vehemently <u>advocates family life</u>. It strongly encourages youth to get married, discourages divorce, and <u>does not regard celibacy as a virtue</u>. That is, almost all marriage-aged women and men are married in an Islamic society. In light of these facts, one would appreciate that Muslim men, in general, have greater financial burdens than Muslim women and thus inheritance rules are meant to <u>offset</u> this imbalance so that the society lives free of all gender or class wars. After a simple comparison between the financial rights and duties of Muslim women, one British Muslim woman has concluded that Islam has treated women not only fairly but also **generously**.

Plight of Widows

1. Because of the fact that Old Testament recognized no inheritance rights for them, widows were among the most vulnerable of the Jewish population. The male relatives who inherited all of a woman's deceased husband's estate were to provide for her from that estate. However, widows had no way to ensure this provision was carried out, and lived on the mercy of others. Therefore, widows were among the lowest classes in ancient Israel and widowhood was considered a symbol of great degradation (Isaiah 54:4). But the plight of a widow extended even beyond her exclusion from her husband's property. According to Genesis 38, a childless widow must marry her husband's brother, even if <u>he is already married</u>, so that he can produce offspring for his dead brother, thus ensuring his brother's name will not die out. "Then Judah said to Onan, 'Lie with your brother's wife and fulfill your duty to her as a brother-in-law to produce offspring for your brother' " (Genesis 38:8).

2. The widow's consent to this marriage is **not required**. The widow is treated as part of her deceased husband's property whose main function is to ensure her husband's posterity. This Biblical law is still practiced in today's Israel. A childless widow in Israel is bequeathed to her husband's brother. If the brother is too young to marry, she has

to wait until he comes of age. Should the deceased husband's brother refuse to marry her, she is set free and <u>can then marry</u> any man of her choice. It is not uncommon in Israel that widows are subjected to blackmail by their brothers-in-law in order to gain their freedom.

3. The pagan Arabs **before Islam** had similar practices. A widow was considered a part of her husband's property to be inherited by his male heirs and she was, usually, given in marriage to the deceased man's eldest son from another wife. The Quran scathingly attacked and abolished this degrading custom: "And marry not women whom your fathers married--Except what is past-- it was a shameful, odious, and abominable custom indeed" (Quran 4:22).

4. Widows and divorced women were so looked down upon in the Biblical tradition that the high priest could not marry a widow, a divorced woman, or a prostitute: "The woman he (the high priest) marries must be a virgin. He must not marry a widow, a divorced woman, or a woman defiled by prostitution, but only a virgin from his own people, so he will not defile his offspring among his people" (Leviticus 21:13-15).

5. In Israel today, a descendant of the Cohen caste (the high priests of the days of the Temple) cannot marry a divorcee, a widow, or a prostitute. In the Jewish legislation, a woman who has been widowed three times with all the three husbands dying of natural causes is considered 'fatal' and forbidden to marry again. The Quran, on the other hand, recognizes neither castes nor 'fatal' persons. Widows and divorcees have the freedom to marry whomever they choose. There is **no stigma** attached to divorce or widowhood in the Quran: "When you divorce women and they fulfill their terms (three menstruation periods) either take them back on equitable terms or set them free on equitable terms; but do not take them back to injure them or to take undue advantage, If anyone does that, he wrongs his own soul. Do not treat God's signs as a jest" (Quran 2:231). "Those of you who die and leave widows should bequeath for their widows a year's maintenance and residence. But if they (widows) leave (the residence) there is no blame on you for what they justly do with themselves" (Quran 2:240).

Polygamy

1. Polygamy is a very ancient practice found in many human societies. The Bible did not condemn polygamy. On the contrary, **the Old Testament and Rabbinic writings frequently attest to the legality of polygamy.** King Solomon is said to have had 700 wives and 300 concubines (1 Kings 11:3). King David is said to have had many

wives and concubines (2 Samuel 5:13). The Old Testament does have some injunctions on how to distribute the property of a man among his sons from different wives (Deuteronomy 22:7). The only restriction on polygamy is a ban on taking a wife's sister as a rival wife (Lev. 18:18). The Talmud advises a maximum of four wives. European Jews continued to practice polygamy until the 16th century. Oriental Jews regularly practiced polygamy until they arrived in Israel where it is forbidden under civil law. However, under religious law, which overrides civil law in such cases, it is permissible. Jesus (P) was not known to have spoken against polygamy. As recently as the 17th century, polygamy was practiced and accepted by the Christian Church. The Mormons (Church of Jesus Christ of Latter Day Saints) have allowed and practiced polygamy in the USA even today. Later regulations fixed the number of wives to 18 for kings and 4 for an ordinary man (Dictionary of the Bible, James Hasting, Charles Scribner's Sons, N.Y, 1963, p624). Monogamy was introduced into Christianity at the time of Paul when many revisions took place in Christianity. This was done in order for the church to conform to the Greco-Roman culture where men were monogamous but owned many slaves who were free for them to use: In other words, 'unrestricted' polygamy. Early Christians invented ideas that women were "full of sin" and man was better off to "never marry." Since this would be the end of mankind these same people compromised and said, "Marry only one." Although the churches do not allow polygamy now, most of Christians are <u>not</u> monogamous. In the western society many times when relations are strained, the husband simply deserts his wife. Then he cohabits with a prostitute or other immoral women (many at the same time) without marriage under the name of 'common law'. **Actually there are three kinds of polygamy practiced in Western societies:**

➢ **Serial polygamy**, that is, marriage, divorce, marriage, divorce, and so on any number of times;

➢ A man married to one woman but having and supporting one or more **girlfriends** (extramarital affairs);

➢ An unmarried man with a number of girlfriends at the **same time**.

2. According to Father Eugene Hillman: "Nowhere in New Testament is there any commandment that marriage should be monogamous or any explicit commandment forbidding polygamy. "Jesus (P) has not spoken against polygamy though the Jews of his society practiced it. Father Hillman stresses the fact that the Church in Rome banned polygamy in order to conform to the Greco-Roman culture (which

prescribed only one legal wife with concubine and prostitution). He cited St. Augustine, "Now indeed in our time, and in keeping with Roman custom, it is no longer allowed to take another wife." African churches and African Christians often remind their European brothers that the Church's ban on polygamy is a cultural tradition and **not an authentic Christian injunction**.

3. The Quran, contrary to the Bible, **limited** the maximum number of wives to four under the strict condition of treating the wives equally and justly. The Quran has "tolerated" or "allowed" polygamy, but why? The answer is simple: there are places and times in which there are compelling social and moral reasons for polygamy. The issue of polygamy in Islam cannot be understood apart from community obligations towards orphans and widows. Islam as a universal religion suitable for all places and all times could not ignore these compelling obligations.

4. In most human societies, females outnumber males. In the USA there are, at least, eight million more women than men. In a country like Guinea there are 122 females for every 100 males. In Tanzania, there are 95 males per 100 females. What should a society do towards such unbalanced sex ratios? There are various solutions, some might suggest celibacy, and others would prefer female infanticide (which does happen in some societies in the world today!). Others may think the only outlet is that society should tolerate all manners of sexual permissiveness: prostitution, sex out of wedlock, homosexuality, etc. For other societies, like most African societies today, the most honorable outlet is to allow polygamous marriages as a culturally accepted and socially respected institution. The point that is often misunderstood in the West is that **women in other cultures do not necessarily look at polygamy as a sign of women's degradation**. For example, many young African brides, whether Christians or Muslims or otherwise, would prefer to marry a married man who has already proved himself to be a responsible husband. Many African wives urge their husbands to get a second wife so that they do not feel lonely. A survey of over 6,000 women, ranging in age from 15 to 59, conducted in the second largest city in Nigeria showed that 60 percent of these women would be pleased if their husbands took another wife. Only 23 percent expressed anger at the idea of sharing with another wife. Seventy-six percent of the women in a survey conducted in Kenya viewed polygamy positively. In a survey undertaken in Kenya, 25 out of 27 women considered polygamy to be better than monogamy. These women felt polygamy can be a happy and beneficial experience if the co-wives cooperate with each

other. Polygamy in most African societies is such a respectable institution that some Protestant churches are becoming more tolerant of it. A bishop of the Anglican Church in Kenya declared that, "Although monogamy may be ideal for the expression of love between husband and wife, the church should consider that in certain cultures polygamy is socially acceptable and that the belief that polygamy is contrary to Christianity is no longer tenable." After a careful study of African polygamy, Reverend David Gitari of the Anglican Church has concluded that polygamy, if ideally practiced, is more 'Christian' than divorce and remarriage as far as the abandoned wives and children are concerned. He personally know of some highly educated African wives who, despite having lived in the West for many years, do not have any objections against polygamy. One of them, who live in the U.S., solemnly exhorts her husband to get a second wife to help her in raising the kids.

5. The problem of the unbalanced sex ratios becomes truly problematic in times of war. Native American Indian tribes used to suffer high unbalanced sex ratios after wartime losses. Women in these tribes, who in fact enjoyed a fairly high status, accepted polygamy as the best protection against indulgence in indecent activities. European settlers, without offering any other alternative, condemned this Indian polygamy as 'uncivilized'. After the Second World War, there were 7,300,000 more women than men in Germany (3.3 million of them were widows). There were 100 men aged 20 to 30 for every 167 women in that age group. Many of these women needed a man not only as a companion but also as a provider for the household in a time of unprecedented misery and hardship. The soldiers of the victorious Allied Armies exploited these women's vulnerability. Many young girls and widows had liaisons with members of the occupying forces. Many American and British soldiers paid for their pleasures in cigarettes, chocolate, and bread. Children were over-joyed at the gifts these strangers brought. A 10 year old boy on hearing of such gifts from other children wished from all his heart for an 'Englishman' for his mother so that she need not go hungry any longer. We have to ask our own conscience at this point: What is more dignifying to a woman? An accepted and respected second wife, or a virtual prostitute as in the 'civilized' Allies approach? What is more dignifying to a woman: the Quranic prescription or the theology based on the **culture** of the Roman Empire?

6. It is interesting to note that in an international youth conference held in Munich in 1948 the problem of the highly unbalanced sex ratio in Germany was discussed. When it became clear that no solution could

be agreed upon, some participants suggested polygamy. The initial reaction of the gathering was a mixture of shock and disgust. After a careful study of the proposal, participants agreed that it was the only solution. Polygamy was included among the final recommendations.

7. The world today possesses more weapons of mass destruction than ever before and the European churches might, sooner or later, be obliged to accept polygamy as the only way out. Father Hillman has thoughtfully recognized this fact, "It is quite conceivable that these genocidal techniques (nuclear, biological, chemical.) could produce so drastic an imbalance among the sexes that plural marriage would become a necessary means of survival.... Then contrary to previous custom and law, an overriding natural and moral inclination might arise in favor of polygamy. In such a situation, theologians and church leaders would quickly produce weighty reasons and biblical texts to justify a new conception of marriage." The same polygamy that they detest and use against Muslims is the very polygamy that they must one day **justify** for themselves!

8. To the present day, polygamy continues to be a viable solution to some of social ills of modern societies. The communal obligations that Quran mentions in association with the permission of polygamy are more visible at present in some Western societies than in Africa. For example, in the USA today, there is a severe gender crisis in the black community. One out of every twenty young black males may die before reaching the age of 21. For those between 20 and 35 years of age, homicide is the leading cause of death. Many young black males are unemployed, in jail, or on drugs. As a result, one in four black women, at age 40, have never married, as compared with one in ten white women. Moreover, many young black females become single mothers before the age of 20 and find themselves in need of providers. The end result of these tragic circumstances is that an increasing number of black women are engaged in what is called 'man-sharing'. That is, many of these hapless single black women are involved in affairs with married men. The wives are often unaware of the fact that other women are 'sharing' their husbands with them. Some observers of the crisis of man sharing in the African American community strongly recommend consensual polygamy as temporary answer to the shortage of black males until more comprehensive reforms in American society at large are undertaken. By consensual polygamy they mean a polygamy that is sanctioned by community and to which all the parties involved have agreed, as opposed to the usually secret man sharing, which is detrimental, both to the wife and to the community in general. The problem of man sharing in the

African American community was the topic of a panel discussion held at Temple University in Philadelphia on January 27, 1993. Some of the speakers recommended polygamy as one potential remedy for the crisis. They also suggested that law, particularly in a society that tolerates prostitution and mistresses, should not ban polygamy. The comment of one woman from the audience that African Americans needed to learn from Africa where polygamy was responsibly practiced elicited enthusiastic applause.

9. Philip Kilbride, an American anthropologist of Catholic heritage proposes polygamy as a solution to some of the ills of the American society at large. He argues that plural marriage may serve as a potential alternative for divorce in many cases in order to obviate the damaging impact of divorce on many children. He maintains that many divorces are caused by the rampant extramarital affairs in American society. According to Kilbride, ending an extramarital affair in a polygamous marriage, rather than in a divorce, is better for the children, "Children would be better served in family augmentation rather than separation and dissolution being options." He suggests that other groups will also benefit from plural marriage such as: elderly women who face a chronic shortage of men and the African Americans who are involved in man-sharing.

10. In 1987, a poll conducted by the student newspaper at the university of California at Berkeley asked the students whether they agreed that men should be allowed by law to have more than one wife in response to a perceived shortage of male marriage candidates in California. Almost all of the students polled approved of the idea. One female student even stated that a polygamous marriage would fulfill her emotional and physical needs while giving her greater freedom than a monogamous union. Few remaining fundamentalist Mormon women who still practice polygamy in the U.S also use this same argument. They believe that polygamy is an ideal way for a woman to have both a career and children since the wives help each other care for the children.

11. It has to be added that polygamy in Islam is a matter of **mutual consent**. No one can force a woman to marry a married man. Besides, the wife has the right to stipulate (in marriage contract) that her husband must not marry any other woman as a second wife. The Bible, on the other hand, sometimes resorts to **forcible polygamy**. A childless widow must marry her husband's brother, even if he is already married, regardless of her consent (Genesis 38:8-10).

12. In many Muslim societies today the practice of polygamy is rare since the gap between the numbers of both sexes is not huge. One can say, safely, that the rate of polygamous marriages in the Muslim world is much less than the rate of extramarital affairs in the West. In other words, men in the Muslim world today are far more strictly monogamous than men in the Western world!

13. Billy Graham, the eminent Christian evangelist has recognized this fact: "...If present-day Christianity cannot do so, it is to its own detriment. Islam has permitted polygamy as a **solution to social ills** and has allowed a certain degree of latitude to human nature but only within strictly defined framework of the law. **Christian countries make a great show of monogamy, but actually they practice polygamy.** No one is unaware of the part mistresses' play in Western society. In this respect **Islam is a fundamentally honest religion**, and permits a Muslim to marry a second wife if he must, but strictly forbids all clandestine amatory associations in order to safeguard the moral probity of the community."

14. Wars cause the number of women to greatly exceed the number of men. In a monogamous society these women, left without husbands or support, resort to prostitution, illicit relationships with married men (resulting in illegitimate children with no responsibility on the part of the father), lonely spinsterhood or widowhood. The society has so many practices that exploit and suppress women, leading to women's liberation movements from the suffragettes of the early 20th century to the feminists of today. The truth of the matter is that monogamy protects men, allowing them to "play around" without responsibility. Easy birth control and easy legal abortion has opened the door of illicit sex with women who have been lured into the so-called 'sexual revolution'. But **the woman** is still the one who suffers the trauma of abortion and the side effects of the birth control methods. Taking aside the plagues of venereal disease, herpes and AIDS, the male continues to enjoy himself free of worry. **Men are the ones protected by monogamy while women continue to be victims of men's desires.** Polygamy is very much opposed by the male dominated society because it would force men to face up to responsibility and fidelity. It would force them to take responsibility for their polygamous inclinations and would force them to protect and provide for women and children.

15. Because of the absence of safety-valve mechanisms, most of the surplus women in post world war Germany indulged in adultery and fornication producing countless illegitimate children. Millions of 'bastards' are being produced every year. The Bible says: "No

bastard shall enter into the assembly of the Lord; even to the tenth generation none of his descendants shall enter the assembly of the Lord" (Deuteronomy 23:2). If a woman, after living a married life for a while finds herself unable to carry on her family obligations because of her inability such as paralysis, insanity or unable to bear children, should her husband kick her out into the street and marry another women? Is it not more humane to keep the women he loves and care for her along with another wife who will be able to fulfill her family obligations? If every man in New York City marries one woman, statistics shows that there will be large number of surplus women without any husband. One option of the surplus is that each observes celibacy the rest of her life. This is not an acceptable option for most of them. She may remain as a girl-friend of any number of men she can manage, having no rights and honor of a wife, producing illegitimate children with no reasonable father to take care of them. When a woman lives with many men which father will be responsible for a particular child? In the western world, taking a woman as a girl friend is the easiest thing for a man. Another option for the surplus women is that she could choose to become a legitimate wife of a man with equal rights, sharing the husband with another woman. Which option will prevent social immorality?

16. **In Islam polygamy is allowed, but under special circumstances and with strict conditions.** This is why most of the Muslims you meet are strictly monogamous. Mohammed (P) was married to one woman, Khadijah, for 25 years. It was only after her death when he had reached the age of 50 that he entered into other marriages to promote friendships, create alliances or to be an example of some lesson to the community; also to show the Muslims how to treat their spouses under different conditions of life. The Prophet (P) was given inspiration from God about how to deal with multiple marriages and the difficulties encountered therein. It is not an easy matter for a man to handle two wives, two families, and two households and still be just between the two. No man of reasonable intelligence would enter into this situation without a great deal of thought and without compelling reasons (other than sexual). The bottom line in the marriage relationship is good morality and happiness, creating a just and cohesive society where the needs of men **and** women are well taken care of. The present Western society, which permits free sex between 'consenting' adults, has given rise to an abundance of irresponsible sexual relationships, an abundance of "fatherless" children, many unmarried teenage mothers; all becoming, among many things, a burden on the country's welfare system. In part, such

an undesirable welfare burden has given rise to bloated budget deficits, which even an economically powerful country like the United States cannot accommodate. Bloated budget deficits have become a political football, which is affecting the political system of the United States. **Artificially created monogamy** has become a factor in ruining the family structure, and the social, economic and political systems of the country. Muhammad (P) directed Muslims to get married or observe patience until one gets married. Mohammed (P) said: "Young men, those of you who can support a wife should marry, for it keeps you from looking at strange women and preserves you from immorality; but those who cannot should devote themselves to fasting, for it is a means of suppressing sexual desire." (This is much safer than joining the "sexual revolution" of the West).

17. Islam wants people to be married and to develop a good family structure. Islam also realizes the requirements of the society and the individual in special circumstances where polygamy can be the solution to problems. Therefore, Islam has allowed polygamy, limiting the number of wives to four, **but does not require or even recommend polygamy**. Today, polygamy in the Muslim societies is not frequently practiced despite legal permission in many countries. In western society, man is getting away without taking responsibility for his actions; Muslim men **do** take responsibility.

18. It is of interest to note that many non-Muslims as well as Muslim countries in the world today have outlawed polygamy. Taking a second wife, even with free consent of the first wife, is a violation of the law. On the other hand, cheating on the wife, without her knowledge or consent, is perfectly legitimate as far as the law is concerned! What is the legal wisdom behind such a contradiction? Is the law designed to reward deception and punish honesty? It is one of the unfathomable paradoxes of our modern 'civilized' world.

The Veil

1. The West sees the veil/head cover as the greatest symbol of women's oppression and servitude. According to Rabbi Dr. Menachem M. Brayer (Professor of Biblical Literature at Yeshiva University), says that for the Jewish woman in rabbinic literature, it was the custom to go out in public with a head covering which, sometimes, even covered the whole face leaving one eye free. He quotes some famous ancient Rabbis saying," It is not like the daughters of Israel to walk out with heads uncovered" and "Cursed be the man who lets the hair of his wife be seen.... a woman who exposes her hair for self-adornment brings poverty." Rabbinic law forbids the recitation of blessings or

prayers in the presence of a bareheaded-married woman since uncovering the woman's hair is considered "nudity". Dr. Brayer also mentions, "During the Tannaitic period the Jewish woman's failure to cover her head was considered an affront to her modesty. When her head was uncovered she might be fined four hundred zuzim for this offense." Dr. Brayer also explains that veil of the Jewish woman was not always considered a sign of modesty. The veil symbolized a state of distinction and luxury rather than modesty. The veil personified the dignity and superiority of noble women. It also represented a woman's inaccessibility as a sanctified possession of her husband.

2. The veil signified a woman's self-respect and social status. Women of lower classes would often wear the veil to give the impression of a higher standing. The fact that the veil was the sign of nobility was the reason why prostitutes were not permitted to cover their hair in the old Jewish society. However, prostitutes often wore a special headscarf in order to look respectable. Jewish women in Europe continued to wear veils until the 19th century when their lives became more intermingled with the surrounding secular culture. External pressures of European life in the 19th century forced many of them to go out bareheaded. Some Jewish women found it more convenient to replace their traditional veil with a wig as another form of hair covering. Today, most pious Jewish women do not cover their hair except in the synagogue. Some of them (Hasidic sects), still use the wig.

3. What about the Christian tradition? It is well known that Catholic Nuns have been covering their heads for hundreds of years, but that is not all. St. Paul in the New Testament made some very interesting statements about the veil: "Now I want you to realize that the head of every man is Christ, and the head of the woman is man, and the head of Christ is God. Every man who prays or prophesies with his head covered dishonors his head. And every woman who prays or prophesies with her head uncovered dishonors her head - it is just as though her head were shaved. If a woman does not cover her head, she should have her hair cut off; and if it is a disgrace for a woman to have her hair cut off or shaved off, she should cover her head. A man ought not to cover his head, since he is the image and glory of God; but the woman is the glory of man. For man did not come from woman, but woman from man; neither was man created for woman, but woman for man. For this reason, and for the angels, the woman ought to have a sign of authority on her head" (I Corinthians 11:3-10).

4. St. Paul's rationale for veiling women is that the veil represents a sign of the authority of the man, who is the 'image and glory of God', over the woman who was created **from** and **for** man. St. Tertullian wrote,

"Young women, you wear your veils out on the streets, so you should wear them in the church, you wear them when you are among strangers, then wear them among your brothers..." Among the Canon laws of the Catholic Church today, there is a law that requires women to cover their heads in church. Some Christian denominations, such as the Amish and the Mennonites for example, keep their women veiled to the present day. The reason for the veil, as offered by their Church leaders, is that "The head covering is a symbol of woman's subjection to the man and to God", which is the same logic introduced by St. Paul in the New Testament.

5. From all the above evidence, it is obvious that **Islam did not invent the head cover**. However, Islam *did* endorse it. The Quran says: "Say to the believing men that they should lower their gaze and guard their modesty...And say to the believing women that they should lower their gaze and guard their modesty; that they should not display their beauty and ornaments except what ordinarily appear thereof; that they should draw their veils over their bosoms...." (Quran 24:30,31).

6. The Quran is quite clear that the veil is essential for modesty, but why is modesty important? The Quran is still clear: "O Prophet, tell your wives and daughters and the believing women that they should cast their outer garments over their bodies (when abroad) **so that they should be known and not molested**" (Quran 33:59).

7. Modesty is prescribed to protect women from molestation or simply, modesty is protection. Thus, the only purpose of the veil in Islam is protection. The **Islamic veil**, unlike the veil of the Christian tradition, is **not a sign of man's authority over woman nor is it a sign of woman's subjection to man**. The **Islamic veil**, unlike the veil in the Jewish tradition, is **not a sign of luxury and distinction of some noble married women**. The Islamic veil is only a sign of modesty with the purpose of protecting all women. The Islamic philosophy is that it is always better to be safe than sorry. Quran is so concerned with protecting women's bodies and reputations that a man who dares to falsely accuse a woman of unchastity will be severely punished: "And those who launch a charge against chaste women, and produce not four witnesses (to support their allegations) - Flog them with 80 stripes; and reject their evidence ever after: for such men are wicked transgressors" (Quran 24:4).

8. Compare this strict Quranic attitude with extremely lax punishment for rape in the Bible: " If a man happens to meet a virgin who is not pledged to be married and rapes her and they are discovered, he shall pay the girl's father fifty shekels of silver. He must marry the girl, for

he has violated her. He can never divorce her as long as he lives'" (Deuteronomy 22:28-30).

9. One must ask a simple question here, who is really punished? The man who only paid a fine for rape, or the girl who is forced to marry the man who raped her and live (miserably) with him until he dies? Which is more protective of women, the strict Quranic attitude or the lax Biblical attitude?

The Modest Dress

1. To the western society, long dress and head cover that the nuns wear represents purity, modesty, dignity, and commands respect. But when a Muslim woman covers her body, **the same society** thinks it represents oppression!

2. Adam and Eve were living in paradise. After being deceived by Satan, they ate from the forbidden tree. They became aware of their physical features and developed the sense of shame. They started to sew the leaves of trees together into a form of dress and covered. (Quran 2:121 & Bible-Genesis 3:7). Although there was no other human being around, it was the sense of shame that dictated him or her to cover them. It is this sense of shame that prevents us from joining many evil activities of society. Animals do not have any sense of shame, which is evident from their total disregard to the time and place of their physical union.

3. Males and females have different physical features, which is one main source of attraction to each other. The physical features are objects of pleasure and lust. Everyone deserves the dignity and respect of a human being, irrespective of their physical features. Human beings are conditioned by the society in which they live. The dress represents modesty, purity, dignity, and through it a woman commands the respect of society. When a man, with desire in his heart, meets a woman who is scantily dressed, or in a tight dress that reveals her physical shape and features, or with deep V-cut blouse showing part of her adornments, his eyes and mind start relishing them. This is simple human nature; God created this reaction. To the man this is something waiting to be explored. To him this woman is giving a signal that she will be available if the time, place, and the price are right. If a person reveals his/her physical features to arouse evil thoughts and desires in another person, he/she is also guilty. Every society houses evil people. In the name of advancement of civilization, social progress, women's rights, and women's liberation, these evil people make slight, subtle and almost imperceptible

changes in the moral and ethical codes of society to **further their own lustful desires**. When society gets used to these changes, they make more changes. Ultimately, some day, one finds that hardly any moral code is left. A look at the western society will reveal some of these consequences (the eastern societies are catching up fast). There are many rampant adultery, countless rapes, millions of illegitimate pregnancies, millions of abortions, and millions of illegitimate children without responsible fathers to care for them. Many of them end up as "street children" joining the gangs and adding to the ever-increasing violence in the society, which has already reached epidemic proportions.

4. When you have a precious gem, you do not leave it exposed anywhere to be taken by others. Rather, you keep it in the best and safest place possible. God made women holy, most dignified, and respectable. They should protect themselves from everything that is evil. Unfortunately women, in general, have allowed the evil society to exploit them. They have made themselves cheap and easily available. They have exposed themselves to the lustful eyes of the society without much hesitation. They have lost their self-respect.

5. In Islam the women are precious and Muslims will go a long way to defend the honor and chastity. The consequence of exposing physical features is very serious and far reaching, both for this world and for the hereafter. It is obvious that both men and women need to cover themselves properly. The main purpose of covering the body is to cover the shame and other physical features so that they remain out of sight of others, will not draw undue attraction, and will not excite evil desires in others. The question is: how much to cover?

Extent of cover

1. God has made women beautiful, and has blessed them with physical adornments. Almost every part of the female body is attractive to a male. Keeping this in mind, the nuns have taken the preventive measure of wearing a veil and covering their whole body, except the face and hands. The Bible says: "For if a woman will not veil herself, then she should cut off her hair, but if it is disgraceful for a woman to be shaven, let her wear a veil" (I Corinthians 11:6).

2. Islam also advises the women to cover their head **and body** except the face and the hands. God says in the Quran:
   - "O ye children of Adam, We have bestowed raiment upon you to cover your shame" (Quran 7:26).

- "Say to the believing men that they should lower their gaze and guard their modesty: they should not display their beauty and ornaments except what appear thereof; that they should draw their veils over their bosoms and not display their beauty" (Quran 24:30-31)

- Mohammad (P) said: "If the woman reaches the age of puberty, No part of her body should be seen but this - and he pointed to the face and hands" (Ref. 40-p6). However, many women cover their faces in public (amongst strange men) as an added means of protection and chastity.

- **The Thickness of materials:** The thickness should be such that no part of the body becomes visible through it.

- **The fitting**: The dress must be loose enough so as not to reveal the shape of body or adornments, which it is supposed to conceal.

- There are people who want to display their wealth through their dresses with pride and vanity. Sometimes God disgraces proud people right before our eyes. Mohammad (P) said: "Whoever drags his clothes (on the ground) out of pride and arrogance, God will not look at him on the Day of Resurrection" (Ref. 8, Vol. 7, #683).

- As the physical adornments of men are much less as compared to women, the dress code for men is less restrictive. However, men must also dress modestly.

- Jewelry is for women. Mohammad (P) forbade gold and silk for men (Ref. 8, Vol. 7, and # 722).

- Men should not imitate women and women should not imitate men. Ibn Abbas narrated that: "Mohammad (P) cursed the men who act like women and the women who act like men" (Ref. 8 Vol. 7, #773).People with responsibility of developing and leading the society, whether they are politicians, civic leaders, Popes bishops, priests, pastors, reverends, movie makers, or media program developers, are actually developing and promoting an evil society. Which of these people will be willing to accept responsibility for sending billions of people to hell as indicated in the Bible?

Women in Hinduism

Sex and Sex-Worship: Hindu scriptures are essentially pornographic in nature, full of sexual allusion, sexual symbolism, passages of frank eroticism, with stories relating to venal love. Some religious sects even introduced ritual intercourse as part of their cult and a potent aid to salvation. The rituals, festivals and ceremonies are characterized by the display of obscene portraits, sex and sex-worship. The temples, places of pilgrimage and other holy shrines are full of sculptures with all sorts of sexual postures. The sexual life of Krishna, an incarnation of Vishnu, is well known for its indecency. He had illicit relations with Radha, wife of his maternal uncle, in addition to a number of milkmaids, although he had a large number of wives. Among Hindu gods, the most prominent ones are: Brahma (the creator), Vishnu (the sustainer) and Siva (the destroyer). Brahma is found guilty of cohabiting with his own daughter, Saraswati. For that reason, he is deprived of being worshipped. Vishnu is guilty of deceitfully ruining the chastity of a married woman, called Tulasi. Siva is not worshipped but the image of his linga (sex-organ) is widely worshipped. This is because of the curse of a sage. In the sculpture, Siva and his consort Parvati are depicted in various explicit poses of the sexual act. Prostitution is encouraged in the form of religious custom of devdasi (slave-girls dedicated to temple-idols). Hindu gods and rishis (sages) are found engaged in sexual acts with beautiful women and breeding illegitimate children. For instance, in order that Rama could have strong soldiers in his army, the gods engaged themselves in begetting powerful sons. This they did by engaging themselves in wholesale acts of fornication, not only against apsaras, who were prostitutes, not only against the unmarried daughters of Yashas and nagas, but also against the lawfully wedded wives of Ruksha, Vidhyadhar, Ghandharvas, Kinnars, Vanaras (monkeys), and produced the vanaras who became the associates of Rama.

Social, Economic and Other Aspects: Caste differences are largely invoked while arranging marriages and eating together. For rural Indians, castes shape almost every aspect of their lives: the food they eat and who can cook it; how they bathe; the color of their clothes; the length of a sari (cloth worn by a woman); how the dhoti (cloth worn by a Hindu man) is tied; which way a man's moustache is trained and whether he can carry an umbrella. Everything is determined by caste and nothing is left to change. Caste regulations formulated by the Manu (system) are discriminatory in nature; they favor the Aryan Hindus and discriminate against the so-called low-caste Hindus. In teaching the duties of the low-caste people concerning marriage, Manu declares that a man aged 30 may marry a girl of 12, and a man of 24 years may marry a girl of 8. He, however, is very particular about the marriage regulations of Brahmans. A Brahman must avoid marrying a girl whose family has produced no sons, that which has thick hair on the body, or is afflicted with hereditary disease. Let him choose for his wife a girl whose form has no defect, who has an agreeable manner, who walks gracefully like a young elephant, and whose body has exquisite softness. Punishment for offence is also determined by discriminatory caste regulations. A crime against a man of his own caste by a Sudra is venial offence; but a similar offence committed against a man belonging to so-called higher caste is proportionately greater. If a Sudra through pride dares to give instructions to priests concerning their duty, hot oil will be dropped into his mouth and ears. A high-caste man having intercourse with a Sudra woman is to be banished; a Sudra having intercourse with a woman of superior castes is to be put to death. Whatever is Brahman's offence, the king must on no account put him to death; he may, at the most, banish him, allowing him to take his property with him. Further, in case of wrongdoing against him, a Brahman need not approach the civil court; he is free to take vengeance upon the offender.

Status of The Sudras: The Sudra has a precarious position in Hindu community. According to Manu Smrithi, a Brahman is forbidden to give advice or even food to a Sudra, for the ghi (clarified butter) having been offered to the gods, must not be eaten by him. Further, the Brahman must not give 'spiritual counsel to him,' nor inform him of the legal expiation of his sin. 'He who declares the law to a servile man, and he who instructs him in the mode of expiating sin, sinks with that very man into hell'. A Sudra is debarred from marrying a woman of the higher castes; if he does, their offspring will sink into a class even lower than his own. He must not participate in carrying the corpse of a Brahman. He is allowed to carry his dead only through the southern gate of the city where he may live. The murder of a Sudra by a Brahman is equal only to killing a cat or a frog or a cow. In fact, the Sudras, who have only deprivations and sufferings in their lots, are not Hindus. The Sudras were not originally part of the Hindu system, but were engrafted into it. Still worse than the Sudras are the Dalits (Untouchables) who fall outside the caste system and are therefore the worst in the social hierarchy.

Inferiority of The Dalit: The so-called Dalits (Untouchables) are the most pitiable victims of the caste system. Manu has little to say about them. He affirms that the members of three castes, the Brahman, the Kshatriya, and the Vashya, are twice-born; the fourth, the Sudra, once-born; there is no fifth.' All others are outcastes. The common name Dasyas (slaves) is applied to them all. The treatment accorded to the Dalit is simply inhuman. According to Manu Smriti: 'Outcasted persons have no share in inheritance.' The orthodox Brahmans still believe, if the shadow of a Dalit falls on them, they are polluted and will have to purify them by sprinkling over themselves water from the holy river, the Ganges. 'You may breed cows and dogs in your house,' writes M.C. Raja. 'You may drink the urine of cows and swallow cow dung to expiate your sins, but you shall not approach an Adi Dravida.' These people are still denied the use of public wells and tanks and at the same time stigmatized as unclean. They are still kept out of schools and colleges maintained by public funds and at the same time despised as ignorant and illiterate. They are still shut out from temples, and yet branded as ungodly and unfit to associate with. For access to public roads and even for spaces to bury the dead, they have to depend much on the capricious benevolence of their caste-Hindu neighbors.

Untouchability in Practice: Untouchability has been banned in the constitution of India, which was drafted by a committee headed by Dr. B. R. Ambedkar, himself an untouchable. It was his great ingenuity that he could tactfully make such a provision in the constitution of a country dominated by the Brahmans. However, there are plenty of evidences that the constitutional provision is honored more by violation than by observance by millions of so-called high caste Hindus.

Sati (Widow-Burning): According to Hindu scriptures, a widow is required to mount the funeral of her dead husband and be cremated along with his corpse. She is called 'sati'. If the husband dies at a distant place, the widow is nonetheless to be burned alive on a pyre by him. Some references from holy scriptures are given below:

➢ It is proper for a woman, after her husband's death, to burn herself in the fire with his corpse; every woman who thus burns herself shall remain in paradise with her husband 35,000,000 years by destiny. The wife who commits herself to fames with her husband's copse shall equal Arundathi and reside in Swarga (heaven).

➢ Accompanying her husband, she shall reside so long in Swarga as the 35,000,000 of hairs on the human body.

➢ As the snake-catcher forcibly drags the serpent from his earth, so bearing her husband with him she enjoys heavenly bliss.

➢ Dying with her husband, she sanctifies her maternal and paternal ancestors and ancestors of him to whom she gave her virginity.

➢ Such a wife adorning her husband, in celestial felicity with him, greatest and most admired, shall enjoy the delights of heaven while fourteen Indras reign.

➤ The practice of widow burning is now made a punishable offenc
This was freely practiced in Hindu States outside the jurisdiction
the British power. The sati, which accompanied the cremation
Maharaja Ranjit Singh of Punjab in 1839AD, is a case in point. 4
his wives and 7 female slaves were burned to death on the funer.
pyre with his corpse when it was cremated. The sati highlights tl
chastity of women. However, when one considers the institution
devdasi (temple prostitutes) to satisfy the lust of the priests and enab
them to earn handsome income through engaging these girls
immoral activities with rich pilgrims, one fails to understand what
the real purpose of sati, upholding the chastity of women, or torturin
them to death?

➤ Today, the alternative of sati is **enforced widowhood**, with all i
degrading accompaniments. It seems as if the Hindu lawgivers mac
harsh regulations to be strictly followed by a widow to make her li:
as miserable as possible. The widow, from the moment of h·
husband's death, not only deplores the loss of a companion, but als
takes a position of utter degradation in the household where formerl
she had an honorable place. In many parts of India, it is customary
few days after the cremation of the husband, to perform the ceremor
of formally degrading the widow, when she has her head shaved t
the barber, deprived of the use of all her personal ornaments, ar
wears plain white clothe (for the rest of her life).

Hindu Women vs. Muslim Women

The Hindu Woman

- The Hindu Woman has no right to divorce her husband.

- She has no property or inheritance rights.

- Choice of partner is limited because she can only marry within h·
  own caste; moreover her horoscope must match that of tl
  intending bridegroom/family.

- The family of the girl has to offer an enormous dowry to tl
  bridegroom/family. In India women die daily of 'dowry deaths
  Hindu women being burned by the husband or in-laws for dowry.

- If her husband dies she should commit Sati (cremated with h·
  dead husband). Since today's law forbids Sati, society main
  punishes her in other "holy" ways by downgrading, isolating h·
  till death such as: a) she cannot remarry; b) she is considered to t
  a curse, c) she must not be seen in public; d) she cannot we;

jewelry or colorful clothes; e) she should not even take part in her *own children's marriage*!

- Marriage must be with his/her cast group.
- Child and infant marriage is encouraged.

The Muslim Woman

- The Muslim woman has the same right as the Muslim man in all matters **including divorce**.
- She enjoys property and inheritance rights. She can also conduct her own separate business (her husband has no rights to her earnings!)
- She can marry any Muslim of her choice. If her parents choose a partner for her, her consent <u>must be taken</u>.
- There is no dowry in Islam. There is a 'marriage gift' from a husband *to his wife*, and **not** the other way around!
- A Muslim widow is encouraged to remarry and start new life.
- Mixed marriage is encouraged and is a means to prevent racism creeping into society.
- A Muslim mother is given the highest form of respect: "Paradise is at the feet of the mother".

How much do people know about Muhammad (P)?

Muhammad (P) was a direct descendent of Abraham (P) through his son Ishmael. He was born on Monday the 12th of the month of Rabi-AlAwwal which corresponds to **August 29, 570**. He received the first message from God through angel Gibrael at the age of 40 in Makka. After that he spent 10 years in Makka and 13 years in Madina to preach Islam; at the age of 63 years he died in Madina. He was unlettered (could not read or write). During these 23 years, the Quran was revealed for mankind. Its original copy in its original Arabic language still exits in Istanbul, Turkey and Tashkent, Uzbekistan. Muslims have been using the same Quran throughout the world since its revelation. Mohammad (P) is the last messenger from God till the last day of this world and his prophethood was for the entire world. Here are some of his sayings:

1. **On God:** He was the most devout in worship to God: "The Prophet used to stand in prayer until his feet became swollen and cracked. He was then asked: 'Hasn't God forgiven you that which is before you and that which is behind you?' He (Muhammad) replied: 'Should I not be a thankful servant?' "

2. **On Life:** Muhammad (P) had a very simple life with minimum worldly possessions. His wife Aisha said: "…we saw three crescents in two months and no fire (for cooking) used to be lit in the houses of Mohammad (P). Someone asked, "Then what was used to sustain you?" Aisha said, "(These two): dates and water." "If I had gold equal to the mountain of Uhud, it would not please me that any of it should remain with me after three nights (i.e. I would spend all of it in God's name) except what I would keep for repaying debts."

3. **On People:** He would joke with his companions, sit and talk with them, and play with their children. "I have never seen anyone who smiled more continuously than Mohammad (P)" (Reported by a companion of the Prophet).

4. **On His Family and Children:** Aisha, his wife said: "He would patch his garments and sole his sandals," She was once asked: "How was he with his family?", she responded: "He was in the service of his family until it was time for prayer, at which time he would go and pray".

5. **On Generosity, Clemency and Conduct:** "The most Perfect believer in respect of faith is he who is best of them in manners."

6. **On Parents:** A man came to Mohammad (P) and said, "O God's Messenger! Who is the most deserving person of my good companion -ship?" The Prophet said, "Your mother." The man said, "Who is next?" The Prophet said, "Your mother." The man said, "Who is

next?" The Prophet said, "Your mother." The man asked for the fourth time, "Who is next?" The Prophet said, "Your father."

7. **On Boundaries of the Religion (humbling himself):** "Do not over-praise me as the Christians over-praised (Jesus (P)) the son of Mary. For I am only His servant, so say: 'God's servant and Messenger' "

8. **On General Mercy:** "A man had laid down his sheep (to slaughter) and then he went about sharpening his knife. Upon seeing this, Mohammad (P) rebuked him saying: 'Do you want to kill it twice? Wouldn't it have been better for you to sharpen your knife before laying it down (so as not to terrorize it)?' " Also, "Mohammad (P) said: 'Pay the worker his (due) wages before his sweat dries' ".

Some famous Quotes about Mohammad (P)

1. The <u>Encyclopedia Britannica</u> states: ".... a mass of detail in the early sources show that (Muhammad) was an honest and upright man who had gained the respect and loyalty of others who were like-wise honest and upright men." (Vol. 12)

2. <u>George Bernard Shaw</u> (famous British philosopher) said about him: "He must be called the Savior of Humanity. I believe that if a man like him were to assume the dictatorship of the modern world, he would succeed in solving its problems in a way that would bring it much needed peace and happiness." (The Genuine Islam, Singapore, Vol. 1, No. 8, 1936).

3. <u>Gandhi</u> says in Young India: "I wanted to know the best of one who holds today's undisputed sway over the hearts of millions of mankind.... I became more than convinced that it was not the sword that won a place for Islam in those days in the scheme of life. It was the rigid simplicity, the utter self-effacement of the **Prophet,** the scrupulous regard for his pledges, his intense devotion to this friends and followers, his intrepidity, his fearlessness, his absolute trust in God and in his own mission..."

4. <u>Michael H. Hart</u> in his recently published book on the ranking of the 100 most influential men in history writes: "My choice of Muhammad to lead the list of the world's most influential persons may surprise some readers and may be questioned by others, but he was the only man in history who was supremely successful on both the religious and secular levels." (The 100: A Ranking Of The Most Influential Persons In History, M.H. Hart, New York, 1978, p. 33).

The Rational Choice

We are raised in the family of our birth and are led to believe that the religion of our family is the best. We believe, follow, and die with this belief, most of us not knowing much about other faiths. It is quite possible that we were born in families with wrong religious faiths. When we attain maturity we should study the different religions, compare them, and then make a **rational choice**. We do not have to follow the religion of our parents if it is not the right one. Prophet Abraham (P) did not follow his parent's religion. "Abraham (P) was not a Jew nor Christian; but an upright Muslim." (Quran 3:67). All children are born in Islam. Muhammad (P) said, "Each child is born in a state of "Fitra", then his parents make him a Jew, Christian or a Zoroastrian...". The Holy Scriptures is the foundation of different religions. Their validity as Holy Scriptures depends on their authenticity. Many authors wrote them, some of whom are known and others are unknown. The Quran is the Holy Scripture of the Muslims. God and angel Gabriel revealed it to Mohammad (P). He then dictated it to the scribes. It is in its original form today in Arabic. **Islam is the final religion of mankind till the last day of this world**. God said in Quran: "We have sent you (Mohammad (P) as a mercy for all nations" (Quran 21:107). "I (God) have perfected your religion for you, completed my favor upon you, and have chosen for you Islam as your religion"(Quran 5:3).

Is it too late?

NEVER!

God said: O Son of Adam...
  ➢ "As long as you pray to Me and have hope in Me, I will forgive you in spite of what you have done, and I do not mind."
  ➢ "If your sins are so many as to fill the sky, then you ask My forgiveness, I will forgive you, and I do not mind."
  ➢ "If you meet Me with enough sins to fill the earth, then met Me while <u>you do not associate any partner with Me</u> (in worship), I shall greet you with forgiveness."

1. Many times the non-Muslim clergies ask their people <u>not</u> to read Islamic literature. Sometimes they even advise them not to discuss religion with Muslims, because they fear that the foundations of their own faith are probably not sound. What kind of faith do they have that it can shatter merely by reading about Islam or talking to a Muslim?

Muslims say: "Read about as many religions as possible, including Islam. You will find the TRUTH in the Quran". They are sure of the Truth and are not afraid to read and compare other religions.

2. Non-Muslims often say that Islam spread by 'the sword'. This is not true. In fact, there is no mention of the word 'SWORD' in the whole Quran. God says: "Let there be no compulsion in religion"(Quran 2:256). No Muslim army went to Indonesia. Only a few preachers went there to deliver the message. Today it is the largest Muslim country. There is not a single TV or Radio Station or a national newspaper owned or controlled by the Muslims in the USA. The media constantly airs negative programs and publishes texts against Islam and Muslims (using billions of dollars). However, these same news medias report that Islam is the fastest growing religion in USA and Europe. More people become Muslims than all the other religious combined together. These include priests, pastors, bishops, doctors, engineers, businessmen, writers, scholars, scientists, social celebrities, people in jail, and 'ordinary' people including a large percentage of WOMEN. There is no Muslim army occupying the USA or Europe, forcing people "by the sword" to embrace Islam. In fact, there are Muslims in every profession including the US Army, Navy, and Muslim Chaplains. Muslim communities are growing fast in every city with over 4,000 mosques in USA and Canada alone. Muslims are contributing in every field along with others and living peacefully in every society. When people come across Islam and see the truth and beauty in it, they become surprised. Their time-old bias against Islam and Muslims, created and nurtured by the clergies and the media, become shattered. They start reading about religions. Very soon they find out that truth lies in the QURAN. It is the force of this truth that convinces people to accept ISLAM.

Conclusion

➡️ Throughout this book, you have seen the harsh realities that women must face. You were also presented with true alternative prescribed for you by God. Do not blindly accept and follow your specific culture, religion, or tradition. Actively **seek out the truth** and have the courage to accept it. You have also seen how different religions were changed, deviated, and distorted from the TRUTH of the original message for various reasons. At the same time anyone who sincerely wanted to find the TRUTH, did find the truth in ISLAM. That is why: Islam is the fastest growing religion in the world. The Truth will **always** prevail as it did time and again. We accept changes everyday to improve and do things in better ways. The US Constitution was written by the founding fathers of the great nation over 200 years ago. Today there are 26 important **Amendments**. God sent different religions at different times and at different places through different Prophets and gradually modified the religion to **suit the needs of mankind**. Islam, being the LATEST REVELATION, addresses all issues for an individual, family, community, state, and the entire world. It has a solution for any problem on the planet. Islam is **A Complete Code of Life**.

➡️ Our stay in this world is temporary (0-120 years maximum); God only knows when the end of this world will come (actually anytime); The Day of Judgment (one day is equal to 50,000 years) is coming soon, and each human being will face God and receive the consequences of his/her deeds forever (infinite years) whether he/she is prepared or not. We came to this world **without choice**; we have to depart **without choice**. But we **have the choice** to find the TRUTH, act on it, and be prepared for the eternal life. You will have this choice until death arrives. **You need to make this decision that will decide your DESTINY**.

➡️ Whether you are a **Hindu, Jew, Buddhist, Christian, Atheist, Communist, Socialist or ANY human on earth**: THE CHOICE IS YOURS. You can see the TRUTH in ISLAM, the Final Religion from the SAME GOD of Moses (P) and Jesus (P). Islam is the final religion for mankind at this time till the Day of Judgment. When the truth arrives in front of you (**as it did just now**), you should **ACCEPT IT** immediately as Abraham (P) did. God said that human beings are His best creation equipped with best sensors to find the best of everything. Let us find the latest and complete REVELATIONS of God: **ISLAM**.

> # Are You Ready to Accept the Truth?

Testimonials: A Wave of Conversion into Islam

Since the events of September 11, Islam has come under intense scrutiny, and as a result people are converting to Islam in greater numbers. Here is a list of number of fascinating news reports, articles, and individual testimonies on this phenomenon before and after:

1. **Islam Converts by the Thousands, Drawn Before and After Attacks**: A must-read story by Jodi Wilgoren, The New York Times [10/25/01] http://thetruereligion.org/afterattack.htm

2. **A Wave of Conversion to Islam in the U.S. Following September 11** - CAIR reports **34,000** conversions (**in 3 months**) since 9/11 [12/01/01] http://thetruereligion.org/convertwave.htm

3. **The Distorted Image of Muslim Women** by Sister Naasira bint Ellison, a convert to Islam http://thetruereligion.org/distorted.htm

4. **Gender Equity in Islam** - PDF format: http://thetruereligion.org/gei.pdf
   HTML version: http://thetruereligion.org/equity.htm

5. **The Status of Woman in Islam** - PDF format http://thetruereligion.org/women.pdf
   HTML version: http://thetruereligion.org/woman.htm

6. **Women's Liberation through Islam** By Mary Ali and Anjum Ali for III&E, http://thetruereligion.org/womenslib.htm

7. **A Woman on a Mission** - Article from *The Guardian* (London) about a Scottish convert http://thetruereligion.org/womanmission.htm

8. **Why Two Women Witnesses?** http://www.spubs.co.uk/daw0014b.htm

9. **Women in Islam vs. Women in the Judeo-Christian Tradition: The Myth & The Reality** http://thetruereligion.org/womenabrahamic.htm

10. **Words to My Muslim Sister** - Heartfelt advice http://www.usc.edu/dept/MSA/humanrelations/womeninislam/advice towomen.html

11. **The Muslim Woman** - Comprehensive site
http://members.aol.com/TheMuslimWoman/Woman.html

12. **Hijab** by Sister Sumayyah Joan, a convert to Islam
http://thetruereligion.org/hijabjoan.htm

13. **My Body Is My Own Business** - Experiences of a veiled Canadian
Muslim woman http://thetruereligion.org/mybody.htm

14. **Why do I wear Hijab ?** by Sultana Yusufali, a 17 year old High
School student http://thetruereligion.org/whyhijab.htm

15. **Rome's envoy to Saudi Arabia Converts to Islam** [11/26/01]
http://thetruereligion.org/italianenvoy.htm

16. **More in Hawaii turn to Islam** [11/26/01]
http://thetruereligion.org/hawaii.htm

17. **"Allah Came Knocking At My Heart"** by Giles Whittell, The
Times. Reports a surge in conversions to Islam since September 11,
especially among highly educated, affluent, young white Britons
[1/8/02] http://thetruereligion.org/ukconverts.htm

18. New Muslims by Marina Jiménez, National Post. Reports on the
increasing propensity of Americans to embrace Islam. **"I really felt
that this religion was the truth and what I'd been looking for my
whole life. I used to feel something was wrong with me because I
couldn't grasp the concept of God. Now I finally had peace of
heart"** - Tiffany Motschenbacher [1/21/02]
http://thetruereligion.org/newmuslims.htm

19. **Islam gains Hispanic adherents in Hudson** [2/3/02]
http://thetruereligion.org/hispanic.htm

20. Concordia students tell of their conversion to Islam [2/8/02]
http://thetruereligion.org/concordia.htm

21. Islam's Female Converts by Priya Malhotra, Newsday.com. **"Islam
represents the beautiful, traditional, grounded and authentic."** -
Marcia Hermansen, Professor of Islamic Studies at Loyola
University, Chicago, USA [2/19/02]
http://thetruereligion.org/femaleconverts.htm

22. **From Christianity to Islam: A Journey of Faith** by Tara Dooley, *Chicago Tribune*. http://thetruereligion.org/journeyfaith.htm

23. A Woman on a Mission - Article from *The Guardian* (London) about a Scottish convert. http://thetruereligion.org/womanmission.htm

24. **Why British Women are turning to Islam** - Article from *The Times* (London). http://thetruereligion.org/britwomen.htm

25. It was as if 'The Scales had been lifted from my Eyes' http://thetruereligion.org/sufyan.htm

26. **From a Bathing Suit to Hijab** by Christine Hauser, *Islamic Voice*. http://thetruereligion.org/bathing.htm

27. Iman finds Islam by Mrs. N. Hashim, *Islamic Voice*. http://thetruereligion.org/iman.htm

28. **Former US Model Overwhelmed by Muslim Pilgrimage.** http://thetruereligion.org/modelhajj.htm

29. **Muslim Women in Japan** - *Japan Times*. http://www.islamzine.com/new-muslims/japan.html

30. **A Japanese Woman's Experience of Hijab** by Nakata Khaula. http://thetruereligion.org/japanhijab.htm

31. **My Transformation to Islam** by Fitra, a recent convert from Osaka, Japan. http://www.islamicvoice.com/november.98/embraced.htm

32. **Small wave of Latinos feel draw of Islam** - *Christian Science Monitor*. http://www.csmonitor.com/durable/1999/08/19/fp17s1-csm.shtml

33. **Converts in Kuwait - From Skirts to Abayas** by Sarah McBride, *Kuwait Times*. http://www.muslim-answers.org/con-kwt.htm

34. **A World Where Womanhood Reigns Supreme (The Seeds of My Own Re-evaluations)** by Mary Walker for the BBC. http://www.muslim-answers.org/marywalk.htm

35. To the Sanctity of Makkah by Fozail Aqdas Ghazali, *Saudi Gazette* - How Rudolph Lewis, a former United States Air Force man, discovered Islam whilst working in Saudi Arabia. http://www.islamicvoice.com/march.99/embraced.htm

36. Muslim faithful are fighting myths that grew out of 9/11 by Andrea Robinson, The Miami Herald [2/21/02] http://thetruereligion.org/fightingmyths.htm

37. Americans in Mecca say Sept 11 Deepened Faith [2/23/02] http://thetruereligion.org/americansfaith.htm

38. Muslims celebrate feast of Eid by Harvey Shepherd, Montreal Gazette. Focuses on recent converts to Islam in Montreal, Quebec (Canada) [2/23/02] http://thetruereligion.org/convertseid.htm

39. The new face of Islam by Nick Compton, *The Evening Standard*. **"All I had ever heard about Islam in the media was Hezbollah and guerrillas and all of that. And here were these really decent people whom I was beginning to get to know. So I started to ask a few questions and I was amazed at my own ignorance"** - Roger, a **British Physician** [3/27/02] http://thetruereligion.org/newface.htm

40. Testimony of Christopher Bohar - A former Satanist (and Christian for some time) from Pennsylvania, USA, was prompted by the tragic events of September 11th to undertake a serious study of Islam: **"I learned that Islam is not a religion of violence or terrorism but a religion of understanding, peace, love, and harmony with God and others"** [3/27/02] http://thetruereligion.org/bohar.htm

41. **Mum, I've decided I want to follow Allah** - Western women are turning to Islam in rapidly increasing numbers. Kay Jardine of *The Herald* discovers why they are so keen to become Muslims [3/19/02] http://thetruereligion.org/mum.htm

42. **"I couldn't be a Muslim! I was American and white!"** - Aminah Assilmi - a former Christian. Faced with losing her husband, children, job, and friends this brave sister never gave up her faith in God and the Truth - and ultimately was rewarded when many members of her family also embraced Islam! She is now well known for her lectures and debates in the USA. http://thetruereligion.org/aminah.htm

43. "'There is no god but Allah,' He has no associates, and all prayers and worship are directed to Him alone. This seemed so simple, so powerful, so direct, and made so much sense" - Akifah Baxter is from a Christian background, and lives in Florida, USA. http://thetruereligion.org/akifah.htm

44. "In Islam I found all that was true, good and beautiful and that which gives meaning and direction to human life (and death)" - Maryam Jameelah (formerly Margeret Marcus) - a well-known writer and convert from Judaism. She also wrote an Open Letter to Her Parents, inviting them to embrace the one true religion. http://thetruereligion.org/mjameelah.htm

45. The Best Way to Live and Die - A touching booklet by (Yahya) Donald W. Flood, an American of Christian upbringing, describing his gradual realization of the solution to 'The Purpose of Life Puzzle' http://thetruereligion.org/bestway.htm

46. The Bible Led Me to Islam - Abdul Malik LeBlanc embarked on a serious study of the Bible, which led him to realize the truth of Islam. His testimony includes a critique of the Bible based on his study, and an examination of Christianity's claims regarding Jesus' divinity, crucifixion and atonement. http://thetruereligion.org/leblanc.htm

47. I Had Not Gone Shopping for a New Religion by Michael Wolfe. An American writer and traveller from a Christian/Jewish background recounts his journey to Islam. http://thetruereligion.org/wolfe.htm

48. Abdullah al-Faruq - Formerly Kenneth L. Jenkins, minister and elder of the Pentecostal Church. http://thetruereligion.org/priests.htm#abdullah

49. Viacheslav Polosin - Former Archpriest of the Russian Orthodox Church. http://thetruereligion.org/priests.htm#polosin

50. Anselm Tormeeda - 14th century CE scholar and priest. http://thetruereligion.org/priests.htm#tormeeda

51. Khadijah 'Sue' Watson - Former pastor, missionary, professor. Master's degree in Divinity. http://thetruereligion.org/priests.htm#sue

52. Ibrahim Khalil - **Former Egyptian Coptic priest.**
http://thetruereligion.org/priests.htm#khalil

53. Anonymous Female Missionary - **Former Catholic missionary.**
http://thetruereligion.org/priests.htm#missionary

54. Martin John Mwaipopo - **Former Lutheran Archbishop.**
http://thetruereligion.org/priests.htm#mwaipopo

55. Raphael - **Former Jehovah's Witness minister.**
http://thetruereligion.org/priests.htm#raphael

56. George Anthony - **Former Catholic priest.**
http://thetruereligion.org/priests.htm#anthony

57. Dr. Gary Miller (Abdul-Ahad Omar) - **Former missionary.**
http://thetruereligion.org/priests.htm#miller

58. Testimony of Dr. Jerald F. Dirks, **a former minister (deacon) of the United Methodist Church.** He holds a Master's degree in Divinity from Harvard University and a Doctorate in Psychology from the University of Denver. Author of The Cross and the Crescent: An Interfaith Dialogue between Christianity and Islam (ISBN 1-59008-002-5 - Amana Publications, 2001). He has published over 60 articles in the field of clinical psychology, and over 150 articles on Arabian horses His testimony can be found at:
http://thetruereligion.org/priests.htm#dirks

| NOW are you ready to accept the Truth? |

References

1. Teachers edition of the Holy Bible, Spencer Press, Inc. 1955.
2. Holy Bible - Revised Standard Version, American Holy Bible Society, 1980.
3. Illustrated Dictionary & Concordance of the Bible - G.G. The Jerusalem Publishing House Ltd., 1986.
4. The Rational Choice, Dr. A. S. Alam, MD; Interfaith Dialogue, POB-0985, League City, Texas 77574.
5. Contradictions and Fallacies in The Bible, by K. Alan.
6. Gospel of Barnabas, Unity Publishing, Cedar Rapids, Iowa, 1980.
7. The Noble Quran – Taqiuddin Hilaly, Dr. Muhammad Muhusin Khan, Darussalam, Riyadh, Saudi Arabia.
8. Sahih Al-Bukhari- Translation by Dr. Muhammad Muhusin Khan, Dar Al Arabia, Beirut, Lebanon, 1985.
9. The New Jerusalem Bible: Introduction to Gospel of John.
10. Ecumenical Translation of The Bible, New Testament - 1972, Pub. Editions du Cert et Les Bergers et les Mages, Paris.
11. Awake, Watchtower Bible and Tract Society of New York, Sept. 8, 1957.
12. The Bible The Quran And Science – Dr. Maurice Bucaille, North American Trust Publication, 1979.
13. Qur'an and modern science Correlation Studies, by Keith L.Moore, Abdul-Majeed A. Zindani, Mustafa A. Ahmed, World Assembly of Muslim Youth.
14. A Scientist's Interpretation of References to Embryology in the Qur'an by: Keith L. Moore, Ph.D.
15. Dictionary of Jewish Biography: Geoffrey Wingoder, Simon & Schuster, NY 1991.
16. Michael H. Hart: The 100, The Ranking of the most influential persons in History.
17. Muhammad in World Scriptures, Dr. Abdul Haq Vidyarthi, Adam Publishers, 1990.
18. Daily Times, London, 25th June 1984.
19. Is the Bible God's word? by Ahmed Deedat.
20. What the Bible says about Muhammad, by Ahmed Deedat.

21. The Choice, by Ahmed Deedat.

22. It is up to you, by Dr. Ahmed Dawood Mizjaji.

23. What is his name? by Ahmed Deedat.

24. Muhummad, The natural successor to Christ, by Ahmed Deedat.

25. Who moved the stone? by Ahmed Deedat.

26. "Muhammad in the Bible", by Prof. Abdul-`Ahad Dawud.

27. "Muhammad in the Bible", Jamal A. Badawi.

28. "Jesus a Prophet of Islam," by Muhammad `Ata ur-Rahim, ISBN 1-879402-07-6 (History of Christianity and the Gospel of Barnabas).

29. "Islam and Christianity in the modern world," by Dr. Muhammad Ansari

30. Muhammad in the Bible, by Jamal Badawi.

31. Let the Bible speak, By Abdul Rahman Dimashkiah.

32. Blood on the cross, by Ahmed Thompson.

33. Christianity, the original and present reality. Dr. Muhammad Abdullah As-Saheem.

34. Christian Muslim Dialogue, by H.M. Baagil, M.D.

35. Islam & Christianity, by U. A. Samad, University o Peshawar, 1988

36. Dimensions of Christianity, Dr. A.H. Qadri, Dawah Academy, 1989

37. Islam, Beliefs & Teaching, Ghulam Sarwar, 1987.

38. Bishya Nabi, by Golam Mustafa, Ahmad Publishing House, Dhaka 1982.

39. The Status of Woman in Islam, Dr. Jamal Badawi, 1972

40. The Muslim Women's Dress, Dr. Jamal Badawi, The MSA of the United States & Canada, May1980.

41. Women in Islam versus Women in the Judaeo-Christian Tradition: The Myth & The Reality, By Dr. Sherif Abdel Azeem.

Informative websites on...

Islam:
http://www.sultan.org
http://www.jews-for-allah.org/
http://islamicity.com/multimedia/radio/
http://islamicity.com/Mosque/uiatm/un_islam.htm
http://thetruereligion.org/
http://alharamain.org/english/truth-seeker.htm
http://www.islam-guide.com/
http://alharamain.org/english/truth-seeker.htm
http://www.it-is-truth.org/Index.shtml
http://www.beconvinced.com/
http://users.erols.com/gmqm/toleran1.html
http://sultan.org/articles/convert.html
http://thetruereligion.org/converts.htm
http://thetruereligion.org/priests.htm
http://www.islamfortoday.com/converts.htm

Family/Women/Children:
http://geocities.com/Athens/Agora/4229/women.html
http://al-usrah.net/
http://troid.org/new/sisters/sistersnet.htm
http://www.muslimmom.com/
http://islamweb.net/english/family/kids/kids.htm
http://216.22.181.137/islam4kids/

Professional/Scientist:
http://www.islamicmedicine.org/amazing.htm
http://www.science4islam.com/
http://islamicity.com/science/
http://sultan.org/articles/QScience.html
http://islamweb.net/english/quran/miracalous/miracalous.htm
http://www.muslimtents.com/muslimguide/1-Science.html
http://www.it-is-truth.org/Index.shtml
salam.muslimsonline.com/~islamawe/Quran/Science/scientists.html

Comparative Religion/Educational:
http://islamicity.com/multimedia/radio/ch200/
http://www.jamaat.net/deedat.htm
http://www.ahmed-deedat.co.za/

Quran:
http://www.quran.org.uk/

Message For All Women...

This book briefly describes various religions brought to this world by different prophets sent by God. All quotations are from holy scripts. Over the years holy scripts were changed, deviated from their original messages. Islam, the final religion sent by the same God of Abraham, Moses, and Jesus remains intact. Its holy book, The Quran, is still available in its original form today. Islam, being the final religion till the last day of this world, addresses all issues for an individual, family, community, state, and the entire world. It has a solution for any problem.

Every human being should study Islam with an open mind and accept the truth. This book has provided enough information for one to judge for him/herself about the truth, without relying on others.

Life after death is very long. There, we have to live forever. Everyday we are using our talents and intelligence to come up with so many innovations, discoveries, and inventions. Why not use these same faculties to find out the latest revelations of God, act accordingly, and be prepared for this eternal life? Many of the images projected by the media are not actual principles of Islam, especially regarding the status of women. We need to be very careful in analyzing for ourselves what God **actually** wants from us. The status of women was downgraded over the years, even in today's western society. Women should try to find out what their own religions say in regards to their status. They should also take an un-biased look into how their own societies and cultures are treating them. Each of us will have to face God on the Day of Judgment and face the consequences of our actions. Each of us is waiting for this long journey. Why not become prepared? Ask yourself: Where am I? Where will I be later? How can I find the truth? How can I prepare? How can I achieve success in the hereafter? All answers are in the final revelations of God: ISLAM.

Copyright © 2002 Madina Masjid, Inc., Houston, Texas.
Library of Congress Catalog Card Number: 2002093030
ISBN: 0-9668190-5-5